DIVINE
EXPECTATIONS

Barbara Kreiger

with Shalom Goldman

Ohio University Press *Athens*

DIVINE
EXPECTATIONS
An American Woman in 19th-Century Palestine

Ohio University Press, Athens, Ohio 45701
© 1999 by Barbara Kreiger
Printed in the United States of America
All rights reserved

03 02 01 00 99   5 4 3 2 1

Frontispiece: Jaffa, looking north. From *Jerusalem and The Holy Land Rediscovered: The Prints of David Roberts (1796–1864)* (Durham, N.C.: Duke University Museum of Art, 1996), p. 229. *Courtesy of Duke University Museum of Art.*

Library of Congress Cataloging-in-Publication Data
Divine expectations : an American woman in nineteenth-century
Palestine / Barbara Krieger with Shalom Goldman.
    p. cm.
  ISBN 0-8214-1294-9 (cloth : alk. paper)
  ISBN 0-8214-1295-7 (alk. paper)
    1. Minor, Clorinda. 2. Missionaries—Palestine Biography.
3. Adventists—Palestine Biography. 4. Missionaries—United States
Biography. 5. Adventists—United States Biography.
    BV3202.M55 D58 1999
    266'.0092—dc21
    [B]
                                                    99-28478
                                                      CIP

To my parents, Elaine and Samuel Kreiger

and in memory of my grandparents
Gertrude and Samuel Chausky
&
Diana and Louis Kreiger

and with memories of my great-grandfathers
Manuel Menachem-Mendel Chausky
&
Abraham Kreiger

Contents

Illustrations

Preface

The challenges of this book were to find lost information from scattered sources; to assemble the various pieces into a coherent form; and to make a narrative where there was none.

Clorinda Strong Minor is an elusive subject. She was probably born in Philadelphia in 1809, but we only know that because she died in 1855 at the age of forty-six. Nothing is known of her life prior to the 1840s. She appeared in the public record in 1843, at the age of thirty-four, then retreated and reappeared in 1849, announcing her plan to go to Palestine. There are no family records of any sort that would provide information on her parents, her childhood, her marriage, her husband, or her son. Nor do we have an image of her face, or a description of her features. She came like a breath into history, lived deeply and briefly, and vanished from records—except for that most indelible record, the one imprinted in memory. For she was remembered, and her work, which has been called a failure, has been remembered. Is success measured by longevity? By numbers of adherents to a cause? By physical evidence? Or could it be that her deeds and her passion created their own terms for judgment of her life? Her motives were inscrutable to most people who knew of her in the United States and Palestine, her inner life a mystery even to those who toiled alongside her. Perhaps it is fitting that, dig as we may, we cannot find her. The genealogies know nothing of her existence, but not so the soil of her adopted land. Would she have wanted more?

Canaan / Hanover, New Hampshire; Jerusalem
winter–spring 1999

Acknowledgments

It has taken some time for me to be able to say with any confidence that I understand Clorinda Minor, and undoubtedly I still don't fully. Conversations with colleagues over the years have been a most valuable part of my work, and I am grateful to others whose work in the historical geography of the Holy Land directly or indirectly helped me in the writing of this book.

I had the honor of knowing the preeminent figure in modern America-Holy Land studies, the late Moshe Davis, who more than anyone helped create this field of study, which hadn't existed before his devoted labor. He welcomed me into his home and shared his thoughts with me, and our conversations gave me confidence that I was on the right track.

Yehoshua Ben-Arieh has done central work in the field; his studies of Jerusalem opened the door for many others and are the basis for much of the contemporary work done on the development of the city since the nineteenth century. I thank him for conversations and fellowship, and for his support.

I am grateful to Ruth Kark for several reasons. As a scholar she has provided numerous articles and books that form a good part of the foundation for detailed investigation of Palestine in the nineteenth century. As a colleague she offered insights and information that furthered my own inquiry. And as a friend she has been a source of encouragement over the years.

For his support over the course of many years and his most helpful and instructive reading of this work, I am grateful to Michael Walzer. I am also grateful to Lester Vogel for his consistent generosity in sharing his views, providing leads, and offering encouragement, as well as for his valuable reading.

I was assisted in my research by the generous help of Patricia Carter in the inter-library loan department of the Baker Library at Dartmouth College. I also thank Marianne Hraibi in that department.

In London I was assisted by the staff of the Public Record Office, and in Jerusalem by the staffs of Yad Izhak Ben-Zvi and the Israel State Archives.

I also thank the Historical Society of Pennsylvania for their research efforts.

Dartmouth College's program for presidential scholars provided research assistants over the course of several years. I wish particularly to thank Linda Albers Serotta, who brought her own great interest and inquisitiveness to the research between 1993 and 1995.

I am grateful to Dartmouth College for the Distinguished Lecturer Award that enabled me to travel to Jerusalem and Jaffa one last time before this book went to print.

I thank Gillian Berchowitz, senior editor at Ohio University Press, for her enthusiasm on first reading my manuscript. Her insights made me feel as though I had conveyed something of what I was after.

I am indebted to Shalom Goldman, whose research propelled my own, whose grasp of the subject's complexities urged me to sharper insights, and whose intellectual energy kept this material fresh.

Finally, I thank my family—Alan, Saul, and Daniel Lelchuk —whose patience and faith became my own.

Note to the Reader

In the last part of the twentieth century, we take it for granted that women and men are referred to in a text by last name only, or by first and last to avoid confusion. In this book, I have decided to do otherwise. The woman about whom I write is Clorinda Minor, yet she was generally referred to as Mrs. Minor. She lived in Palestine as Mrs. Minor; took on the British government and commanded the attention of the Ottoman authorities as Mrs. Minor; and she died as Mrs. Minor, her name inscribed: "Mrs. C. S. Minor . . . Philadelphia, U.S.A."

Calling her "Minor" serves contemporary taste, but seems inauthentic. I honor her for who she was, and will let others judge my choice.

Note on Spelling

In narratives of nineteenth-century travel in Palestine, the spelling of names and items varies a great deal, as can be expected, since English-speaking writers transliterated the Arabic or Hebrew according to how they heard it. Generally the variation is not confusing; Beyroot is readily seen as Beirut, and Joppa is recognized as Jaffa. Occasionally, though, especially when the place is not familiar, the inconsistency can be misleading for those who are unaccustomed to Arabic or Hebrew sounds. The name of the village where the first half of this story takes place is often written as Urtas, but appears also as Artas, and it is the latter that I have chosen to use.

DIVINE
EXPECTATIONS

❨

Introduction

I N RECENT DECADES the United States has become so involved in the Middle East that it is easy to forget that a
strong commitment there dates only to the middle of this
century. The United States was a relative latecomer to the region;
several European nations had hovered over the expiring Ottoman
Empire in the nineteenth century—even as they propped it up—
waiting for the right moment to land. Recent as the American
commitment is, however, it has its roots in the first part of the
nineteenth century, when American missionaries and travelers, propelled by religious imagination or a sense of adventure, were beginning to define the East as their meaningful territory at the same
moment that most of their contemporaries at home were looking
west. In fits and starts, with naiveté and bravado, the American
connection to the region called the Holy Land began to take shape.
If those early efforts were largely failures, whether to establish
missions, introduce modern agriculture, or stake out a diplomatic
presence, they did serve as the necessary foundation on which a
substantial structure was gradually erected.

Americans had long been engaged in the Levant. Beginning in the Colonial period, they traded in Ottoman territory under the British flag, and though it would be some time before they reached the shores of Palestine in any significant way, it was inevitable that eventually they would press on. In the 1840s steamships brought Alexandria to within a month's travel from New York, making the additional journey to the Holy Land somewhat less daunting. By the 1860s American-accented English was commonly heard in Jerusalem.

In the 1820s, the American Board of Commissioners for Foreign Missions tried to install a missionary in Palestine, but conditions there were unfavorable in every respect, and the attempt failed. The next decade was more encouraging, with the Egyptian ruler Mohammed Ali temporarily in control of Palestine. Under his rule, a tentative toehold was gained, yet the American missionary presence in Jerusalem was short-lived for various reasons. England and Prussia established a dominating Protestant presence, and the American Board shut down its mission and withdrew to Beirut.

In Jerusalem, the Americans lagged diplomatically as well. In 1831 the United States concluded a treaty with the Ottoman Turks and established a ministry at Constantinople. Consulates were opened in several places of relative importance, such as Alexandria and Beirut, but Jerusalem received little attention. Finding qualified personnel was not an easy matter; generally no Americans were available to serve anywhere in Palestine, so the assignments were offered to local merchants, a situation that offended the national sentiments of some American travelers and was not, in any case, the most effective way of promoting American interests. In 1844 the United States was embarrassed when an American citizen, duly appointed but quickly dismissed as consul to

Jerusalem, set up an office there and "served" his nation for two years before stepping down. Except for this fiasco, Jerusalem remained without an official American presence until 1857. American travelers and residents were invited to enjoy the protection of the British consulate, which had been in operation since 1839 (followed within a few years by Prussia, France, and Sardinia), but farsighted individuals knew it was a mistake to leave the small and vulnerable American population of the Holy Land dependent on British largesse. Indeed the first real consul was appointed too late to assist a small American settlement that for four dramatic years had cried out to Washington for help.

At the center of the story is a Philadelphia woman named Clorinda Strong Minor, a spiritual seeker and millennialist who actively promoted the idea of the restoration of the Jews to their ancestral land. In the decade before the American Civil War, Mrs. Minor led a small, fervent group of believers to Palestine. With no agricultural background, she established a colony to introduce modern farming methods and to teach the Jews of Jerusalem and Jaffa what she herself was just learning. Her work had a significant, if largely forgotten, effect on agricultural settlement in Palestine through the next decades.

Before her first voyage to Palestine, in 1849, Mrs. Minor played a part in an American drama of divine expectations. In the 1840s she was a follower of William Miller, a charismatic preacher who proclaimed the imminent advent of Christ. The 1844 failure of Miller's prophecy and the ridicule heaped on tens of thousands of his followers sent Mrs. Minor into an emotional and spiritual tailspin. She emerged transformed from her crisis, firm in the conviction that it was not the soil of North America that needed her commitment, but the soil of Palestine. A kind of maverick millennialist by that point, she declared that she would devote her body as well as her soul to the reclamation of the land—decades before European Jewish pioneers established a network of farming communities in Palestine, half a century before the First Zionist Congress in 1897 formally articulated the Jewish idea of "redemption of the land," and several critical years before the United States realized the importance of a strong diplomatic presence in that part of the fading Ottoman Empire.

Clorinda Minor's vision and the life she defined for herself were singular, and the place she came to occupy was way out on the periphery of Protestant circles. Yet her faith that the world would be saved by sudden divine intervention placed her in the thick of things. There was widespread belief both in England and Germany in the late eighteenth and early nineteenth centuries that the Second Coming was approaching, and in the United States millennialism also found fertile ground. By the 1830s, the idea that the Millennium, the thousand-year reign of Jesus and his followers, was drawing near was embraced by many Protestant groups. Contrary to their opponents' claims, the believers in imminent salvation were not all uneducated, and a broad socioeconomic spectrum was represented in their membership. At church services, prayer meetings, and revivalist rallies, the believers were exhorted to prepare for the end of time. It was assumed that a remnant of the Jewish people would return from their exile to the Land of Promise, where they would "see the light" of Christianity and stimulate the redemption.

Despite her thoroughly Christian beliefs, Mrs. Minor, oddly enough, held views that corresponded to those of some of the most forward-looking Jews in America when it came to the question of Jewish restoration to Palestine. In 1845, the prominent Jewish politician and journalist Mordecai Manual Noah published his "Discourse on the Restoration of the Jews," twice delivered to large, influential Christian audiences the previous year. The essence of his address was a request for assistance in returning the Jews to the Land of Israel. Citing a letter he had received nearly three decades earlier from "the illustrious author of the Declaration of American Independence," Noah recalled Thomas Jefferson's words: "'Your sect, by its sufferings, has furnished a remarkable proof of the universal spirit of intolerance inherent in every sect, disclaimed by all when feeble, practiced by all when in power; our laws have applied the only antidote to this vice . . . but more remains to be done, for . . . public opinion erects itself into an inquisition, and exercises its office with as much fanaticism as fans the flames of an auto-da-fe.'"

Former President John Adams echoed Jefferson's view when he wrote to Noah, "'I wish your nation may be admitted to all the privileges of citizens in every part of the world. This country has done much; I wish it may do more.'" But while Jefferson was not speaking to the idea of actual Jewish restoration to Palestine, Adams was: "'I really wish the Jews again in Judea, an independent nation. . . . [O]nce restored to an independent government, and no longer persecuted, they would soon wear away some of the asperities and peculiarities of their character.'" Although Adams added that, in time, with these "peculiarities" diminished, the Jews might become "liberal Unitarian Christians," his restoration sentiments were clear.

In his "Discourse," Mordecai Noah made a remarkable appeal for the Jews' physical return to Zion. And if it was not fully practical—"We must not stop to ask whether the Jews will consent to occupy the land of Israel as freemen. Restoration is not for us alone, but for millions unborn"—his argument was deeply felt. "Let the people go," he urged; "point out the path for them in safety, and they will go, not all, but sufficient to constitute the elements of a powerful government; and those who are happy here may cast their eyes towards the sun as it rises, and know that it rises on a free and happy people beyond the mountains of Judea." Addressing the practical issues, Noah asked that Christians solicit permission from the Sultan for Jews to purchase land and to follow in full security any occupation they desired. He prodded his audience with a reminder that according to Scripture, the "great events connected with the millennium" will only take place after the restoration of the Jews: "You believe in the second coming of Jesus of Nazareth. That second advent, Christians, depends upon you. It cannot come to pass, by your own admission, until the Jews are restored, and restored in their unconverted state." As though to make his plea more appealing, he invited Gentiles to become "better acquainted with the Jew. . . . See him in the bosom of his family, the best of fathers, and the truest of friends. See children dutiful, affectionate. . . . See wives the most faithful, mothers the most devoted."

In his expression of hope for a return to Zion, Noah was within the mainstream of Jewish thought. Where he departed from the mainstream was in his call for political action to bring about restoration. (Similar ideas were propounded by the European rabbi Zvi Hirsch Kalischer, who saw the Jewish settlement of Palestine as a precondition of the redemption, not as its consequence.) Noah's statement reached a fair-sized Jewish audience and drew a mixed response. Even so, the Jewish community in the United States, which by the 1840s numbered roughly twenty thousand, did not have the power to pursue grandiose plans.

The notion that the Jewish people were an intimate element in the redemptive process, even if there was no agreement about their exact role, was manifested in newly founded evangelical societies. In 1820, a quarter century before Mordecai Noah published his plea, a new organization boldly announced its purpose in its name, The American Society for Evangelizing the Jews. (The name was almost immediately toned down to the less threatening American Society for Meliorating the Condition of the Jews.) The Society was founded in an attempt to convert a Jewish population of a mere few thousand, and its membership included a large number of distinguished citizens, such as John Quincy Adams. Its actual success in converting Jews was very minor; indeed it has been suggested that the Society may have frightened Jews with its aggressive intentions, thereby helping to fashion them into a cohesive community.

Beyond the religious sphere, there was a strong inclination among some Americans to respond to the situation of the Jewish people on a moral level. Thomas Kennedy immigrated to the United States from Scotland and was elected in 1817 to the House of Delegates in the state of Maryland, where Jews were barred from public office and legal practice. Kennedy had never met a Jew, but he asserted that one's religion "is a question which rests, or ought to rest[,] between man and his Creator alone." He became the leader in the struggle over the next seven years to pass a bill—called the Maryland "Jew Bill"—that would repeal the test oath that excluded Jews and would "extend to the sect of people professing the Jewish religion, the same rights and privileges that are enjoyed by Christians." So consummately devoted was Kennedy to the cause of political equality that he went so far as to declare: "[I]f Christianity cannot stand without the aid of persecution . . . let it fall; and let a new system, more rational and benevolent, take its place."

Focused though he was on domestic politics, Kennedy also had something to say about the future of the Jewish people beyond the shores of the United States. Like many of his contemporaries, he observed the decline of the Turkish empire and interpreted world events as moving toward a dramatic new order: "[I]f we are Christians indeed and in truth, we must believe that the Jewish nation will again be restored to the favour and protection of God. . . . though scattered and dispersed in every country. . . . their future state will no doubt be more glorious than ever. . . . [M]ay we not hope that the banners of the children of Israel shall again be unfurled on the walls of Jerusalem on the Holy Hill of Zion?"

The connection between the fate of the Jews and political events drew more attention in the next two decades. In 1840, the Jews of Damascus were accused of using Gentile blood at their Passover seder. This recurrence of the ancient blood libel resulted in the persecution of the Jews of Syria and at the same time helped activate Jewish and philo-Semitic opinion in the United States and Europe. Along with the general millennialist feeling that held sway at the time, the Jewish question was brought to the forefront of political discussion.

❡

And so we return to Clorinda S. Minor, one of the least known, yet most pivotal, figures in the story of the evolving American connection to Palestine, the Holy Land, a land holding well under half a million inhabitants in the mid-nineteenth century. As we shall see, when Mrs. Minor made the decision to settle in Palestine in 1852, it was because she saw herself as a participant in the unfolding divine drama. Whether she was familiar with the argument put forth by Mordecai Manual Noah is not known, though the timing of events did allow for it. It is clear that she believed that the restoration of the Jews to Palestine and the reign of Christ were intimately linked. Acting on this belief, she became one of the key figures in the agricultural development of Palestine. Beyond this, she was the unwitting catalyst for a revision of American policy in the region, as the long conflict in which she was embroiled while in Palestine, and its aftermath, exposed the inadequacy of American diplomatic representation there.

At any other time in American history, Clorinda Minor's eccentric view of herself as God's messenger might have remained merely quaint, and would have had no implications for the Jews, Palestine, or American diplomacy. History offered her an opportunity far more down-to-earth than the one she conceived of for herself. The chance correspondence of her life with certain significant world events laid the groundwork for one of the most unusual chapters in the history of the American connection to the Middle East.

Part I: Artas

☾

The Hebrew seers announce in time
The return of Judah to her prime;
Some Christians deemed it then at hand.
Here was an object: Up and do!
With seed and tillage help renew—
Help reinstate the Holy Land.

Herman Melville, Clarel, A Poem and Pilgrimage
in the Holy Land, *1876 (I, xvii, lines 261–66)*

one

☾

Clorinda Minor, and
Arrivals in Palestine

I N MAY 1849, aboard a merchant ship headed for the Mediterranean, a forty-year-old Philadelphian, her teenage son, and
a companion posing as her brother were embarked on the
first leg of their journey to Palestine. Weak with motion sickness,
Clorinda Minor finally managed to walk on deck and make the
first entry in the journal that would eventually be published as
Meshullam! or, Tidings from Jerusalem. How, she wondered, had she
come to be "a weary stranger, a pilgrim on the sea," far from home
and friends she loved? There was no obvious answer to the question, so improbable was it that the wife of a sedentary businessman should have left her comfortable life and subjected herself to
all the uncertainties that now defined her existence. From an early
age, when she lost her devout mother, Clorinda (then Strong) was
a self-described seeker of God who, despite her membership in
the Congregationalist Church, felt unfulfilled by conventional religious practice. Forty years after her death, Clorinda Minor was
described by the custodian of her letters as a "mystic by nature,

an enthusiast by temperament," one who "gloried in martyrdom" and unconsciously longed "to actualize her individuality in such a role." But what did that have to do with Palestine?

❆

Millennialism had been a growing force in America during the 1830s. Though many preachers spoke and wrote of the impending eschaton, however, few ventured to fix a date for the final unfolding of the cosmic drama. One who dared to do so was William Miller, a Baptist preacher who in a series of lectures published as *Evidence from Scripture and History of the Second Coming of Christ About the Year 1843*, announced that his long study of the Scriptures led him to calculate the time of the last days. Miller's appeal was largely to Baptists and Methodists, and by 1842 he had around fifty thousand followers, one of whom was Clorinda Minor. Mrs. Minor had done her own study of the prophetic portions of the Scriptures, and after hearing Miller sermonize about the imminent End of Days, she found her religious imagination clasped in a grip that would not be loosened for the rest of her life.

So sure were his followers of Miller's authority that they did not plant their fields or send their children to school, some even selling their homes in order to support his cause. When 1843 passed with no apparent cosmic consequences, the movement's leaders concluded that they had used the wrong calendar for their calculations, and they refigured the approaching revelation based on the Hebrew calendar. Yom Kippur, "the tenth day of the seventh month," was to be the day of redemption. That year, the Day of Atonement would fall on October 24–25. The divine plan was plain for all to see.

"This shop is closed in honor of the King of kings," scrawled one businessman on his window shutter; "get ready, friends, to crown him Lord of all." The believers met for days before the an-

This "warning," submitted by Clorinda S. Minor, appeared in the *Philadelphia Public Ledger* on October 10 and 11, 1844. Courtesy of the Historical Society of Pennsylvania, Philadelphia, Pennsylvania.

ticipated Apocalypse, praying in small chapels from early morning until late at night. Mocked by a gathering rabble, the congregation of some two hundred men, women, and children sought refuge outside the city. Several "sad parting scenes" were witnessed at various locations in Philadelphia as the groups prepared to set out. Parents were reported to have left their small children; grown children persuaded aged parents to follow; a carpenter canceled building contracts; some sold their houses and threw the proceeds into the general fund; one man tossed a large sum of bills and coins into the street, where it was quickly gathered and pocketed by local children. Bidding farewell to the "Sodomites of Philadelphia," the congregation climbed into wagons and headed to their hillside encampment. (It was reported that "large parties of these insane people" were also encamped at several other locations along the Schuylkill River and around the city.) In the sanctuary of their tent, they began their prayers and vigil. A newspaper correspondent described the unusual sequence of events, watching as one "highly respectable citizen" came searching for his wife and finally convinced her to go home, despite "terrible threats of Divine vengeance" thrown at him by other congregants.

Clorinda Minor, later described as "the high prophetess of

that religious delusion called Millerism," led the congregation in prayer, then withdrew to the rear of the tent with her husband and son, her watch open in the palm of her hand. The designated hour passed, and night fell. At midnight the faithful were dozing when a terrible storm struck, tearing roofs off houses and uprooting trees. The tents of the encampment were whipped to shreds; panic-stricken women and children ran screaming. Two small children froze to death, one woman was insensible, and many others were suffering so severely that residents of the neighborhood of Phoenixville literally forced some of them into their houses in order to save them. By morning many of the congregants had returned to the homes they thought they had left forever, and bore the scorn of neighbors who asked derisively if they had forgotten their umbrellas and galoshes.

Printed reactions ranged in tone from scornful to patient. "People addle their brains and sacrifice their duties for an idiot's dream," wrote one observer. "Millerites," he exhorted them, "attend to what we are saying. You will all die fast enough, and you need be in no haste to expedite the mysterious business of an unknown world." Another commentator looked for a bright spot, noting that with the return of the misguided victims to their homes, it seemed the delusion had partly subsided. This journalist's hope was that the authorities would check any new attempt to mislead and deceive these sincere people, in case some rogue was waiting to take advantage of their weakness. Conciliatory, he urged humane people to help dispel the illusion, now that "the time" had gone by, and to show kindness in order to restore the minds of the mistaken. Yet though Miller's predictions were discredited, he remained a powerful force, and a year later, Millerites of "generally respectable . . . appearance," were still being baptized in the Schuylkill River. When Miller died in 1849, millennialist ardor was barely diminished among the members of the sect that had come to be called Adventists. The Seventh-Day Adventists, an outgrowth of Miller's original group, modified the radical views of their founder by setting no specific time for the Second Coming. As one early twentieth-century observer noted, they were thus spared the "perpetual disappointments" of their predecessors.

Clorinda Minor, meanwhile, was sheltered solicitously by her husband and son. For weeks she fasted, prayed, and examined the prophecy in an effort to discover where their error had been made. Crushed by Miller's failure, she slid into a physical and psychological decline. Two years later she emerged with an explanation, one which placed her well outside Millerism and set her on a solo course in vast, uncharted waters. In a reworking of Christian typology, according to which New Testament parallels are found for the exemplars of the Hebrew Bible, she announced that she was Esther, summoned by God to go to Mount Zion and "make ready the land of Israel for the King's return."

When Mrs. Minor embraced Millerism, she had effectively divorced herself from her religious circle, amid "bitter censure and stinging ridicule." She knew that this new decision to go to Palestine meant she could very well lose everything—home, family, community—but she could not ignore the call of her inner voice. Her journal offers no comment about her husband's attitude, as she began raising money for the trip. Charles A. Minor, a conventional man who must have been greatly befuddled by the turn his marital life had taken, had stood by her until this moment. But exasperation overpowered forbearance, and he refused to help finance his wife's trip. Then, in a shocking development, a fellow believer, one John Boyd, announced that he too was called to the Holy Land and would accompany Mrs. Minor. The only thing stranger than this nearly illicit arrangement was the fact that neither believer's spouse protested, at least not publicly. Whether their acquiescence was sincere or feigned cannot be known. Perhaps their anxieties were allayed by the fact that the third pilgrim was to be Mrs. Minor's teenage son, Charles Albert, Jr.; or perhaps they had perfect faith in the mission. Then too, it might have been that to voice vain objections would only have exposed their helplessness in the face of this new ardor, which one could only hope was solely divine.

Still short of the full fare, the travelers planned to go to New York, wondering how they would proceed from there. But Providence took charge; Mrs. Minor talked too long with friends, and they missed the train. That night, stranded in New Jersey, she saw a note advertising the departure of a merchant vessel to Marseilles, and they booked passage for half the expected price. On May 15, 1849, the trio set sail for Palestine. In God's hands or not, they were on their way.

Rain and nausea were Mrs. Minor's companions for almost the full month of their Atlantic crossing, but she kept rebounding with observations that marked her as a woman of distinctive sensibility. On sighting Africa, she lamented the fate of Africans: "My heart weeps for thy wrongs, Oh, Africa! the sunny home, our Father once gave to his dark-browed children, who now, by their brethren's hand, are homeless and bound!" Her antislavery sentiment corresponded to her attitude toward the Jews of Palestine, of whom she would speak in similar terms five years later.

As they sailed past Cape Trafalgar, her thoughts turned to her long dead father, who had once been captured by Barbary pirates and held for ransom. His vessel seized, he had been carried to Algiers and condemned, then rescued and restored to his family. Contemplating human history, Mrs. Minor emphatically denounced as "legalized murder" all the wars that had bloodied the seas. Yet the pacific scene calmed her, and the familiar note it struck offered comfort: "The sand, rocks, and irregular hills, bear the same Maker's impress as those in our own dear land. The sky is just as blue and bright, and the white clouds, in beauty float above, the very same, as in the long June days they rest over the green banks of the Schuylkill and Delaware." After the excitement of the last few years, she was taken by the tranquillity which surrounded her; how strange it was, "this almost vacuum of existence!" But her mood swung from day to day with the stress of the trip. By the time they landed at Marseilles in early July, her journal, filled with expressions of love for God, was also punctuated with supplications. It is the diary of an overwrought and exhausted individual.

Mrs. Minor and her son and John Boyd took rooms in a large house, and she inquired about the way to Palestine. But her French was meager, hardly anyone spoke English, and no one, including the American consul, knew any more about Jerusalem than she did. Eager to flee the place that was to her nothing more than the site where Protestant martyrs had shed their blood resisting the attempts of the Catholic church to convert them, she was firm in her resolve to get to the Holy Land, affirming that just one Jewish soul needing help would justify her mission. Unannounced, a young man came to their door and in broken English said he had heard of their plight and wished to help. Characteristically, Mrs. Minor commented that he obviously had been sent by God: "While we feel the most sincere gratitude and esteem for him, we *know* that it is *the Lord*, that has sent him to our relief."

A few days later they prepared to leave for Alexandria on an English mail steamer. Actually, just the two adults were continuing on, as Mrs. Minor's son had become ill and was returning home —an apparently straightforward matter, yet one which was later said to have had a poisonous effect on future events. Leafing through Mrs. Minor's diary and correspondence half a century later, the trustee of her papers reflected cryptically on the young man's departure: "Nor was there a breath of suspicion on the part of the husband and wife at home: a dreadful mistake of course, in Mrs. Minor's career, and disastrous in its final consequences; but in their innocence they did not dream that they could be censured. As brother and sister they went on their way—and were known on the rest of the journey as Mr. and Miss Adams. Had they not Abraham to justify them if needs be?" For readers of the Bible this was a familiar scenario. In Genesis 12 Abraham tells the Pharaoh that his wife Sarah is his sister. The story is repeated in Genesis 20, when Abraham, acting out of fear, again misrepresents his marital status to Abimelech, king of Gerar. The patriarchal precedent must have bolstered Mrs. Minor whether or not her relationship with John Boyd was conjugal.

Bidding farewell to their American captain, they watched as their heaviest trunk, while being hoisted over the side of the vessel, was dropped and sank. To the sailors' great surprise, but not to Mrs. Minor's, it rose to the surface inexplicably and was promptly snagged and retrieved. There were very few passengers in the heat of the summer, but their budget required them to purchase second-class accommodations, where it was stiflingly hot. They changed boats in Malta and headed for Alexandria as Mrs. Minor struggled vainly against the heat until the captain offered her a first-class berth with a porthole and an awning outside. It was the so-called sickly season, a time of cholera related to the inundation of the Nile River. Landing in Egypt during the seasonal epidemic would cost weeks of quarantine on arrival in Palestine, so crew members were not permitted to disembark in Alexandria, but Mrs. Minor did. She called on the American consul, who was startled to find her traveling in the perilous season. Contrary to her expectations, the English mail steamer to Jaffa did not take passengers, especially not when a quarantine was in effect. The consul called on his Arab assistants to help them, and lodging was arranged in an Italian house. The heat, anxiety, and fatigue were too much for her, and Mrs. Minor collapsed with dysentery.

While she was confined to bed, a new acquaintance searched for a steamer. There was no regular communication with Jaffa, and no prospect of a vessel for a month. A French steamer to Beirut stopped regularly, but had left a few days before their arrival; the only vessel due to sail for Beirut was a small boat laden with rice, with neither cabin nor awning. Mrs. Minor considered her prospects. Beirut was a good hundred miles from Jaffa, but it would be far easier to reach Jaffa along the coast of Palestine than from Egypt. Signing on, they waited while their friend scurried around town buying furniture and provisions. And credit has to be given to this Philadelphia lady, who with tentative good cheer prepared to sail: "This is a new way of traveling, but I will hope all things, and venture forward."

Hope aside, the scene which awaited her as they made their way to the boat in Alexandria harbor was something her imagination had not prepared her for. Two Arabs carried their baggage, and they rode on donkeys as half-covered men and boys crowded around, all seeking to do some service that would merit reward. "The scene was like a strange caricature; Ali brandishing his plated staff . . . with one hand, and holding a string of crying chickens in the other, going before to turn aside the droves of laden camels, mules, and donkeys that were pressing upon us in the mingled crowd." With these human waters parting, they approached the dock, but the first view of their boat prompted Mrs. Minor to confess she could "scarcely describe" her sensations. It was small, had no bulwarks, and was so heavily laden with human beings seated on rough matting which covered the cargo of rice that it sat just a few feet above the water. A spot was cleared in the center, and they deposited their baggage under the astonished gaze of their neighbors. They could communicate with no one, and when their assistant left, they were consigned to total isolation. There they sat holding their umbrellas "in suffering suspense" until the captain, dark-skinned and turbaned, made his appearance with the long boat. Mats were spread, and a low tent was erected for them. They could not stand, but sat like the others on the floor, their trunks at one end, their large basket with provisions and cooking and table apparatus at the other. They were equipped with quilts and carpet bags and cloaks, which would serve as bed, pillow, and sofa.

While waiting for the wind to signal their departure, Mrs. Minor observed the human crowd in the harbor. It was Ramadan, the month-long Muslim fast, and a number of the Pasha's great warships were about, each colorfully bedecked. The passengers, Greeks, Moors, Egyptians, and Arabs, offered a most picturesque sight, with their variety of complexions, features, and dress. She took care to describe both sexes, observing of the veiled women that the poor creatures were "scrupulous to obey this absurd law of human fashion!" One cook served them all; in the evening, melons, squashes, beans, lentils, and rice were all boiled together as thick soup that was served in wooden bowls with pieces of dark bread. Families ate together—men, women, children, and slaves sitting on mats and dipping in alternately with their fingers. After the meal they began the "most piteous chanting," not in concert but each on his own, sounding to her like an unearthly wail. Yet rather than scoff at the din, Mrs. Minor ascribed religiosity to her strange companions; she interpreted the wailing as "sincere, devotional aspiration," and did not hesitate to join in. The next day they were out to sea, a gentle, reviving breeze thrusting them toward the coast of Palestine.

During the voyage, Mrs. Minor met a poor Jew who was returning from Algiers to his family, and they communicated as best they could in a combination of French, Italian, and English, while he began to teach her Arabic. He waited on them, trying to make them comfortable and conveying their culinary requests to the cook. For dinner they had chicken boiled with rice, and Mocha coffee morning and evening. Bread, raisins, and oil accounted for the rest of their diet. Their neighbors were kindly, and everyone participated in her Arabic lessons by bringing her an assortment of objects. Several suffered from eye afflictions, and in the tradition of western travelers in the Near East, she offered them ointment for treatment.

Progress was slow, as the winds were light and unpredictable. When a contrary wind rose one day, the captain ordered the sails trimmed, but in spite of his efforts, the vessel was spun frustratingly around toward Egypt. Finally, more than a week into the voyage and seventy-three days after leaving Philadelphia, they sighted the coast south of Beirut. The breeze which propelled them was too light for landing, so at dawn the next day they were awakened and transferred to a smaller boat which was towed in closer. Their yellow flag of quarantine raised, they dropped anchor at noon and waited while the captain went ashore to bring an officer to clear them for entry. Mrs. Minor was near fainting under the hot sun. No food was available, and the Nile water they had brought was beyond drinking. After some time, a large boat arrived to ferry them to shore. She was relieved to escape from the vermin which plagued their shipmates, but to her dismay all the bedding was thrown on top of theirs, and the passengers came crowding around them. A young Greek who wished to thank her for the eye ointment sat down next to her; in horror at the "creeping plague" on his garments, she protested his proximity, but to no avail. Before the boat banged up against the rocks, their new friend Solomon sprang out and whisked her in his arms to the beach, a gracious welcome, she thought, from a son of Abraham.

In Beirut everyone was taken to the quarantine quarters, rows of low rooms on a point overlooking the harbor. A guard was appointed to keep them from escaping, hardly a necessary precaution since Mrs. Minor was again incapacitated with dysentery. Solomon made her a bed from mats and her quilt and cloak, and the availability of charcoal meant they could boil rice and make coffee. The bread must have been entirely inedible since she chose instead to pick through her old worm-infested crackers; soaked in sweet oil and accompanied by rice, they constituted her diet. Mosquitoes and fleas abounded, and lizards crawled on the walls. Mrs. Minor managed to write to her consul and request help in reaching Jaffa when the quarantine was over, but his reply was discouraging; an English ship sailed monthly, but it would leave before their quarantine was ended, so she would have to wait another month. Dysentery and fever were raging in the city, and she was distressed at the prospect of staying beyond the necessary time, especially when an English doctor told her that fatalities were higher than in fourteen years. There was one comfortable hotel in town where she might find relief, but she could not afford it.

Finally Mrs. Minor's prison-like room was unlocked and two Arabs proffered a note from the American consul instructing that she and her companion be put aboard an Arab *felucca* going to Jaffa. She was so weak that she could barely get to the boat. After rowing a mile in the sun, they reached a small open craft, with neither deck nor awning. A few dark, wild-looking men, naked except for a short apron-like garment around the waist, cleared a spot

Bay of Beirut. From *Picturesque Palestine, Sinai, and Egypt,* ed. Colonel Wilson, R.E., C.B., F.R.S., with numerous engravings on steel and wood from original drawings by Harry Fenn and J. D. Woodward (New York: D. Appleton and Co., 1883), vol. 2, after p. 34.

amid the ballast for her mat to be spread. Pain and fatigue left her helpless, and she lay down under her umbrella. Solomon brought water and hung some pieces of mat over her. In anguish she contemplated the voyage to Jaffa and assumed she might die before landing. That evening, as if in a dream, she heard her name called out by an English-speaking voice from a boat which drew up alongside theirs. At the helm was an American captain who had heard of their plight and had been searching for them all over the harbor; he invited them to board his ship, which happened to be the first American merchant vessel ever to visit Beirut. It had arrived from New York in a mere thirty-seven days, a voyage so improbably short that Mrs. Minor assumed it must have been divinely assisted: "Our moaning prayer was turned into thanksgiving and joy, as if an angel had been sent down from heaven to our relief! We received it as the direct interposition of our heavenly Father." In a further coincidence, though probably unknown to Mrs. Minor, one of the passengers aboard that ship was J. Horsford Smith, a businessman who would soon take over as the American consul in Beirut, and someone who would play a major role in the events of her life over the next few years.

The next morning the captain received them warmly and advised them to feel at home with his wife and young daughter until the steamer sailed. Mrs. Minor bid a reluctant farewell to Solomon and expressed the hope of seeing him in Jerusalem. Then she concentrated on getting well, with the help of fresh milk, eggs, fruit, cakes, and breads, not to mention peace of mind. As she mended, she spent several evenings in Beirut, on one occasion meeting Sir Moses Montefiore, the English Jewish philanthropist, who was returning from Jerusalem. He offered practical advice about her trip, and she was much impressed by the "Jewish nobleman." Thinking about Jerusalem, Mrs. Minor reflected on the number of Christians who visited "the classic remains of pagan philosophy, of *deified* men and heroes, whose elevation mostly consists in the greatest number of men conquered! enslaved! butchered!"—and how few visited the land where Jesus walked and preached. Recalling the epithets thrown at her over the years, she mused that a visit to the classical lands is esteemed, but a visit to the Garden of Gethsemane is regarded by the Christian world as "enthusiasm and *fanaticism!*"

Mrs. Minor's travel problems were not yet over, but just when she was wondering how she would manage to reach Jerusalem once they landed at Jaffa, tragedy struck the captain and his wife, and her question was answered. On a trip up into the mountains of Lebanon to see the American missionaries, their little girl contracted dysentery and died, and the grieving parents decided to make Jerusalem their destination. Soon after arriving at Jaffa, they all set out for the two-day journey as part of a twenty-animal caravan that included a missionary and his daughter, a young Turk, and a few Arab travelers. They rested briefly the first night at an Armenian convent in Ramleh, midway between Jaffa and Jerusalem. The moon was up before one in the morning, and they were off again toward the mountains, with more "natives" joining them. As they picked their way along, Mrs. Minor noticed details of her surroundings—several threshing floors stacked with piles of wheat and chaff, and Arabs lying asleep without blankets or pillows; occasional gardens of melons and cucumbers enclosed within careless piles of stones, with a little hut in the center. At daylight they reached the lower terrace of the mountains of Judea. It seemed impossible to find a path leading up the steep, stony hills, but rains had chiseled a rough defile whereby one animal at a time could pass. Up they climbed, three thousand feet, and suddenly there was Jerusalem before them, the physical reality tempering Mrs. Minor's customary effusiveness: The city's "formidable and ancient walls and towers," she wrote in her diary, "its lofty minarets and domes, give it an air of peculiar solemnity and grandeur!"

The group entered at the Jaffa Gate, as Turkish soldiers bowed. Mrs. Minor and her companion set out to find accommodations, but there was only one hotel in the city, and prices were high. After a serpentine trek beneath arched corridors, they finally located it but learned that the hotel was closed in the off-season, and that the proprietor, John Meshullam, was in Bethlehem with his family for the "sickly," or hot, months. Mrs. Minor was exhausted and hungry, and much confused. One of their escorts demanded a messenger be sent to Bethlehem to inform the innkeeper that a number of important guests were waiting. In three hours Mr. Meshullam arrived and saw to their comfort. With their minds on food and

Inside the Jaffa Gate, Jerusalem. From *Picturesque Palestine, Sinai, and Egypt*, ed. Colonel Wilson, R.E., C.B., F.R.S., with numerous engravings on steel and wood from original drawings by Harry Fenn and J. D. Woodward (New York: D. Appleton and Co., 1883), vol. 1, p. 1.

rest, no one could possibly have foreseen what bearing this chance meeting would have on the future of nearly everyone in the room.

Meshullam's staff put rooms in order, and by mid-afternoon they were sitting down to an elaborate dinner of bread, grapes, figs, wine, soup, mutton, and home-grown potatoes and tomatoes. A few days later Mrs. Minor's American acquaintances returned to the coast, and Meshullam invited her to stay with his family. His youngest son, Peter, just fourteen, would be their interpreter, and one of the other sons, either Elijah, who worked in the English hospital, or James, who had just returned from school in London, would guide them to the holy places. For a small price Meshullam also agreed to provide donkeys for excursions. Arrangements made, they began exploring.

A visit to the Holy Sepulcher turned depressing when a crowd of beggars pressed around Mrs. Minor, making it impossible to finish her sketching, but most of her excursions were more rewarding. One day they left the city by the Damascus Gate and followed the walls around to the east. They descended into the Kidron Valley, from where they could see a cluster of dark old olive trees enclosed by a plastered wall, a garden that Mrs. Minor knew intuitively to be Gethsemane. Later she obtained permission to enter, a privilege which the Latin Convent had just bought from the Turks. Another day trip took her past the Pillar of Absalom, where many small stones were heaped, thrown in contempt by passing Jews in a traditional response to the rebellious son of King David, an old custom designed to inculcate respect for parents. According to a seventeenth-century French Catholic pilgrim, the inhabitants of the Holy City would bring their children to the tomb of Absalom "to shout and throw stones at it, stressing the end of wicked children who did not revere their parents." The practice was apparently shared by Muslims, but one English resident reported that the Arabs he saw throwing stones explained they did it only because Absalom was a Jew.

Another day they left the city by way of the Jaffa Gate, Mrs. Minor noting that the walls on the west side were more regular and beautiful than elsewhere. One morning she went out St. Stephen's Gate to climb the Mount of Olives. The view was the "most affecting to me of any that earth can give," she wrote. Jerusalem lay below, with the broad, level Temple site, circled by trees and fountains; above to the left were the lofty terraces of Zion, with the sealed gates, waiting silently for the Messiah to come. She imagined the ruins and the Dome of the Rock gone, and in their place a rebuilt Temple, with Jesus reigning.

When Mrs. Minor was confronted with the religious past, her journal narrative became a string of ejaculations and devotional outbursts. But when she was face to face with mere surface reality, she reported detail and impressions in a simple and effective way that alerts a reader's senses to daily life in the city. The narrow streets were paved with uneven stone worn glossy by the ages. She noted the absolute darkness of Jerusalem's passageways at night, since house windows did not open onto the street. She called Jerusalem "a city without wheels," and remarked that the darkness and stillness of the streets increased the awe that brooded over the somber walls at night. At midnight the stillness was interrupted by a sound like distant thunder, and it took her some time to identify the noise. It was the sound of countless millstones, turned by women who labored at night and continued until morning, as the work was too taxing in the heat of the day. Mrs. Minor herself tried to move a stone, but could scarcely manage a small one. A woman needed to grind an hour per night in order to obtain enough flour for each family member's daily bread.

After a short stay, Mrs. Meshullam took Mrs. Minor and her

Women grinding with a stone mill. From *Buried Cities Recovered, or, Explorations in Bible Lands,* by Frank S. DeHass (Philadelphia: Bradley, Garretson, & Co., 1882), p. 136.

companion to Bethlehem by donkey, their mattresses, furniture, and baggage loaded on camels. They squeezed through narrow alleys between small stone houses built into the side of a hill and stopped at a low door. Stooping to fit through, they entered the Meshullams' courtyard and ascended to their apartment. As she got to know him, Mrs. Minor was obviously greatly taken with John Meshullam, and her imagination was stirred as she regarded the life he had made for himself in Palestine. She claimed that "his whole heart and hope is in the good of his poor brethren [i.e., the Jews] and the restoration of Zion"—a somewhat ironic aspiration, given his conversion to Christianity and the fact that the rabbis in Jerusalem, fearing a missionary threat, had to a large extent forbidden Jews to have anything to do with him. Most significant to Mrs. Minor was the fact that Meshullam's religious commitment was coupled with cultivation of the land. He had been farming for several years and was quite successful despite lack of tools and seeds, severe seasonal changes, and the difficulty of applying modern tilling techniques with unschooled help. She and her companion visited his little farm southwest of Bethlehem, near the village of Artas (or Urtas in many travelers' accounts), and she was impressed by both the rugged, unplanned beauty—fig trees growing among the cliffs, terraced pomegranates, lemon and olive trees, grape vines—and by Meshullam's careful labor—young orchards of peach and pear trees, fields of tomatoes, cauliflower, beets, eggplant, beans, onions, and wheat.

Toward the end of September, on Yom Kippur, Mrs. Minor left Bethlehem with Mrs. Meshullam to reopen the hotel in Jerusalem, an odd profanation of the most sacred day on the Jewish calendar given that Mrs. Minor's feelings about the Jewish condition were unquestionably genuine. When she observed "the last remnant of Jehovah's ancient and chosen people," she felt both sorrow and reverence. After all the years, she reflected, through centuries of misery and captivity, they still recalled the unfulfilled promises, and taught them to their children. Still, her compassion was the sort the saved feel for the unregenerate, and as the Jews praised their God, she praised her King of the Jews.

On a visit to the Jewish Quarter Mrs. Minor found her friend Solomon sick again and living in a common home for the poor. He lay listlessly on a mat on the stone floor, with only an old blanket to cover him. There was no space for him in the hospital, so Elijah

Meshullam brought him medicine. Mrs. Minor was astounded by the general squalor and misery in the Jewish Quarter, an observation made by numerous others and substantiated by a contemporary view of the Jews of Jerusalem in mid-century. Elizabeth Ann Finn, the activist wife of James Finn, then the British consul, noted that when she and her husband arrived in 1846, there were around seven thousand Jews in Jerusalem, about a third of the total population. More than half were Sephardic, with family origins in Spain and Portugal, northern Africa, and central Asia. They were permitted to settle on the eastern slopes of Mount Zion and for a fee could pray at the Western Wall. Many of them were carpenters and glaziers and spoke Ladino, a mix of "old Spanish" and Hebrew. They never went beyond the city walls except for the monthly prayers at Rachel's tomb, and were extremely poor.

The Ashkenazi numbered three thousand, some of whom had been driven to Jerusalem by the Russian persecutions. A good number were elderly and had made their way by being passed along by fellow Jews from town to town along the route to Palestine. Among them were watchmakers, jewelers, carpenters, and tailors —"hundreds of willing Jewish artisans," James Finn wrote, who "were obliged to exist in compulsory idleness, and chronic starvation." They were largely dependent on money collected for their support in Europe, but Mrs. Finn asserted that as early as 1846, this *chalukah* fund was markedly insufficient for their needs. The language of the Ashkenazi was Yiddish, but Mrs. Finn observed in her *Reminiscences* that Jewish men from Kabul, India, and Jerusalem, meeting as total strangers, at once conversed in Hebrew, "still a thoroughly living language, for speaking as for literary and religious purposes."

Poor health was widespread among the Jews, and Mrs. Finn recalled that in 1847 a newly arrived English doctor offered the opinion that lack of food and consequent malnutrition caused their vulnerability to disease. He persuaded Mrs. Finn that the prevalence of eye afflictions could be attributed to a meat-deficient diet, a situation Mrs. Finn attempted to allay by distributing small portions of kosher meat every Friday to insure a Sabbath meal. Further, she reported that poor Jews came in large numbers to the British consul for help. She tried to create some small employment for the women by giving them sewing and knitting, but could not provide work for all of them. In 1848, a young English missionary, Caroline Cooper, arrived to work for the Anglican Church. Along with Mrs. Finn, Miss Cooper devised a plan to employ poor Jewish women in needlework. Soon they had thirty women working, but the rabbis got alarmed, Mrs. Finn reported, and warned the women to stop. They left, but soon returned; eventually a hundred and fifty women were employed in what came to be called the Sarah Society.

The need for employment seems to have been extensive and unremitting by the summer of 1852. The Finns had planted a vineyard as a source of employment, but it was not ready to be worked, so they employed a number of Jewish men clearing stones and building at Talbiyeh, located just outside the city, where the Finns had their summer encampment. The year 1854 was very hard for Jerusalem's Jews. In the midst of the Crimean War, the Russian government had stopped all money coming from Jews in Russia to their families in Palestine, because the practice was seen as aiding Russia's enemies, the Ottoman Turks, who ruled Palestine. Furthermore, there was a food shortage because of a prolonged drought, and prices were rising. James Finn explained that the Christian poor were helped by their communities, and the Muslims extended hospitality to one another; only the Jews had no reserves or wealthy brethren, and the *chalukah* fund was virtually exhausted.

That winter, 1854, water should have been plentiful, since the rains had filled most of the cisterns in the city. But in the Jewish Quarter, because the houses were rented, the cisterns had been allowed to fall into disrepair, meaning that the Jews had to buy water that was carted in from springs outside the city. "The state of poverty among the Jews at this time," Consul Finn noted, "exceeded anything we had before known." Yet still, Mrs. Finn claimed, the rabbis tried to forbid the Jews to work in the vineyard, where roughly two hundred men were then employed; she claimed they were even driven with whips back to the city, the Ashkenazi chief rabbi asserting that they were not permitted to work for Christians.

To what degree the Jewish leadership actually prevented Jews from working for Christians is not clear. Yet the threat they perceived to their community was real, and hardly a secret. The rabbis' experience was that the poverty of the Jews was often exploited by Christian missionaries who would in effect exchange bread for baptism, and they were understandably suspicious. Employment of the Jews and missionary work were closely linked in the efforts of most Protestants, many of whom believed that the restoration of the Jews to the Holy Land and their conversion to Christianity were prerequisites for the Second Coming. In 1838, the London Society for the Promotion of Christianity Among the Jews authorized the purchase of land and construction of an imposing Protestant church in Jerusalem. Defined as a chapel for the British consulate, in keeping with Ottoman regulations, Christ Church was completed in 1849. As a missionary tool, the church's importance was obvious. Mrs. Finn's father, for example, the eminent Hebraist Alexander McCaul, had advocated such a project some years before; it would demonstrate to the Jews that the English Church, unlike the Eastern Orthodox and Roman Catholic Churches, did not worship images, meaning that conversion to the Protestant

Church was not an embrace of idolatry. Physical relief was not always, and not clearly, tied to conversion, but deprivation was a factor in the perceived susceptibility of the Jews to Christian missions. Whether the enterprise was subterfuge or not, the allurement was obvious.

And where was the American Protestant establishment all this time? There had been American missionaries in Palestine in the 1820s and '30s, but by the 1840s their activity had declined, partly because of denominational squabbles, but also because of intense competition. In 1841, Britain and Prussia agreed to the establishment of a joint bishopric in Jerusalem, a venture that marked a serious effort by the Protestant body to establish themselves against the Roman and Eastern Orthodox churches, while also making a statement about growing Russian influence. The first bishop, Bishop Alexander, formerly Michael Solomon Alexander, was himself a converted Jew, and probably had been appointed with that strategic element in mind, a ploy which did not go unremarked by Mordecai Noah, who scoffed at the compounded insult of using a Jew to convert Jews in the Jews' sacred city. On Sunday mornings, Bishop Alexander conducted an English service, followed by one in German and another in Hebrew.

During the 1840s and '50s, European powers, through their consular offices, struggled to improve their positions with regard to the holy places. In Jerusalem the status of those holy sites was both a cause for intervention—and created the need for it. Russia claimed the right to oversee the Orthodox holy monuments, France made the same claim over Catholic ones, and Britain assumed the right over the Protestant ones—which they built so that they could protect them. It is not that religious activity was merely a pretext, but all the jockeying for position did have to do with a lot more than religious matters. Religious influence was an important element in the struggle for political standing; with the demise of the

Ottoman Empire just a matter of time, and with the Russians on the horizon, the stakes were very high.

By the time the new bishopric was established, the Americans had more or less conceded Jerusalem and relocated in Beirut, where their work led to the founding of the Syrian Protestant College, later the American University of Beirut. In 1849 American Christian missionaries made a renewed effort in Palestine, but without much success. The consequence of the American Protestant establishment's powerlessness in Jerusalem at this time was an absence of American political influence that would be very costly to Clorinda Minor and her fellow settlers.

Clorinda Minor, who for all her religious aspirations was not part of the missionary community, realized that her short stay in the Holy Land had defined a new goal for her life. The trip had originally been intended as a simple pilgrimage; but having viewed the poverty which plagued the Jews of Palestine, Mrs. Minor was beginning to formulate a vision that, in her mind at least, was supported by John Meshullam and the agricultural work in which he was engaged. For someone as intent as she on recognizing the workings of Providence, her chance acquaintance with Meshullam, a converted Jew working the land, must have been too powerful a coincidence to ignore. Her calling, amorphous yet insistent, and possessing her since young adulthood, was finally taking form in the agricultural prospects she suddenly found presented to her. She had only to grab this opportunity and trust in God. The rest would unfold when she presented her scheme at home and convinced others that their donations to her cause would insure them a share in Paradise.

Even the very soil knew the promise was about to be fulfilled. The land, "in harmony with the improving prospects of its scattered people, is showing symptoms of returning to *life.*" Thousands of Jews, she exclaimed, were confined to the fetid alleys of the cities, with no work, rarely emerging, sickly, poor, "their weak animal existence scarcely sustained by a rigid charity, and dragging out a suffering existence, in all the horrors and destitution and ignorance; and this in their own land." For a small expense, she insisted, they could do agricultural work and be raised and liberated to a blessed position.

According to Mrs. Minor, John Meshullam was made hopeful by her enthusiasm, yet had learned to be skeptical about professed commitment; others, he told her, distinguished men of piety, had come and promised their help, yet when they left, the misery faded from their eyes and they forgot Meshullam's appeal. Would she also forget? Mrs. Minor replied that were it not for a promise to return home and report on what she found, she would stay even then. If it were God's will, she would return, and bring with her fellow believers from home. Departure time was approaching, and all the while Mrs. Minor had been suffering from chills and fever. But as her ship was to leave on November 3 and it was already the end of October, she had no chance to recover before setting out. Meshullam made careful arrangements for her comfort, and she traveled to Jaffa suspended in a pannier from the side of a mule as Meshullam and Solomon, the latter much recovered and intent on learning to farm when she returned, escorted her out of Jerusalem.

Mrs. Minor left Jerusalem on November 1, 1849, and for months was silent. It took seventy-two days to get to England from Jaffa, and she was sick every day until Christmas. The weather was terrible, the provisions coarse, the captain unprincipled and severe. Reduced to the lowest state of existence, she was unable to sit up for an hour during the entire voyage, and she despaired of life. At last the ship arrived in England, where she was invited to a sympathetic home to recuperate. It was two months before she could travel again, but Mrs. Minor felt her suffering was rewarded when she met someone who agreed to act as postal intermediary between herself and Meshullam, since there was no direct communication between the United States and Palestine.

Finally she set sail on the last stretch of her journey, five months after leaving Jerusalem. In the mid-Atlantic they experienced a violent storm, the likes of which the captain hadn't seen in all his fifty years on the sea. The ship survived, and, Jonah-like, Mrs. Minor was delivered at last onto American soil, prepared to tell what she had seen. Her journey ended, her story was about to begin.

❨

On her return to Philadelphia in the spring of 1850, Clorinda Minor, by then apparently a widow, began the work that would enable her to return to Palestine and join John Meshullam at Artas. She must have spent some time propagating her ideas, because the record of donations, dating from the very month she landed in the United States, reveals that money was already coming in, if in small quantities, from Maryland, New York, and Connecticut, as well as from Philadelphia. In May, June, August, September, November: $25, $10, $5, two pieces of gingham, a book on farming—the contributions trickled in, from "a friend," "a lady," a "lover of Israel." Slowly, slowly, $256 was accumulated and was spent on shovels, hoes and rakes, seeds, medicine, and a plow.

Things were moving along at a steady pace. Meshullam wrote to thank Mrs. Minor for the cabbage seeds that had arrived from England and for the flour mill which was promised by an English benefactor. In June she sent the first large shipment from the States, and in November Meshullam wrote that he was glad to have received the mill, though the people who needed it were too weak to use it. Their plans progressed steadily, even if there were intimations that all was not rosy in Jerusalem, where "some deleterious stupor," as Meshullam called it, was blinding certain individuals to the worthiness of their enterprise. Meshullam affirmed that he believed in his new colleague's good intentions, and he repeated five months later that from the first, he had trusted that she was motivated only by "Christian beneficence." The admiration was mutual, as each poured compliments over the other and expressed total faith in the other's pledge.

Who was this enigmatic figure who was at the center of the American experience in Palestine? In a case where little unanimity on any point is to be found, we can start with John Meshullam's very name. It is likely that he was originally named Meshullam—a common Hebrew name—son of whatever his father's name was, and that when he converted he adopted the Christian name John and changed his given name to a surname. Meshullam was probably born in London around 1800, the son of wealthy and religious Greek Jews. When the boy was four years old, his father took the family and set sail for Jerusalem. At Cadiz, the elder Meshullam learned of Bonaparte's Mediterranean embargo, which had virtually cut off access to the eastern Mediterranean. Meshullam's father sold the boat and went by land to Salonika, the northern Greek port city, where he planned to stay until events favored travel.

Salonika, or Thessalonika, was the seat of an ancient and distinguished Jewish community, the origins of which went back to the time of the Greco-Roman empires. The majority of its members were Sephardic, their ancestors having come from Spain and Portugal after the mass expulsions of the late fifteenth and early sixteenth centuries. In the first years of the nineteenth century, Meshullam's father would have found a thriving Jewish center of some thirty thousand people. The city was important in trade, and Jews played a large role in the export of grain and textiles. Salonika was also famous as a center of rabbinical studies, particularly in the areas of *halakha* (the body of laws that governs Jewish life) and mysticism. Salonika had been under Turkish rule since 1430, but

MESHULLAM!

OR, TIDINGS

FROM JERUSALEM.

FROM THE JOURNAL OF

A BELIEVER

RECENTLY RETURNED FROM THE

HOLY LAND.

Comfort ye—comfort ye, my people,
Saith your God—speak ye comfortably,
To Jerusalem and cry unto her,
That her warfare is accomplished!

Isaiah xl, 1, 2.

PUBLISHED FOR THE AUTHOR.

1850.

The title page of Clorinda Minor's book, first published in 1850, *Meshullam! or, Tidings from Jerusalem* (Philadelphia, 1850). Courtesy of the Library of Congress.

with the decline of Ottoman power in the early nineteenth century, long-felt resentment against Turkish authority erupted into violence. The movement that would eventually lead to Greek independence took the form of armed insurrection against the Turks. In one such revolt, Meshullam's father, mother, brothers, and sisters were murdered, probably because Salonika's Jews had sided with the Turks in their long occupation. For reasons that are unclear, young Meshullam had earlier been sent back to London to attend a Jewish school.

The boy stayed in London and continued studying until the age of fifteen, when the rabbis and an uncle tried to "force him," if Mrs. Minor is to be believed, to "become one of their number" and hand over to their common fund the wealth he had inherited from his father. The headstrong teenager refused and went to Berlin, where he continued his studies. At nineteen, he revisited Salonika, perhaps to reconstruct the events of his family's murder. In the synagogue, Joseph Wolff, a converted Jew and energetic missionary, angered the congregation by addressing them on the subject of the Messiah. Meshullam used his influence to intercede on Wolff's behalf and saved him from the irate crowd.

From there, Meshullam, still a believing Jew, went to Jerusalem, where he remained for three years, traveling and learning Arabic. He hoped to fulfill his father's dream of settling there, but was restless, purposeless, and homeless, and he extended his travels to the East, through Europe, and possibly to the Americas, learning a dozen languages along the way. Several sources identify Meshullam as the guide of the poet Robert Byron in Greece. Chronological and geographical factors seem to support the claim, but it is problematic because the purpose of Byron's second trip to Greece, the trip that corresponded to Meshullam's itinerary, was to participate in the Greek struggle for independence, a struggle that Meshullam might have been hard-pressed to support, since it had brought about the murder of his family.

Finally Meshullam returned to London, where he heard that Joseph Wolff was to preach. Meshullam had never before been in a church, but was curious to see Wolff again. Wolff, a German Jew originally, made England his home and had joined the Church of England. He worked for the London Jews Society, zealously seeking to bring his "unenlightened" brethren into the fold of the true religion. Wolff preached to Jews wherever he could, but as his notoriety preceded him, he increasingly had to avoid Europe and seek out more distant Jewish communities. When Meshullam entered the church, he was recognized and introduced to the congregation as the very young man who had saved Wolff's life in Salonika three years earlier. Listening to Wolff talk about the coming of Christ, Meshullam, though plagued by doubt and guilt, was further intrigued.

Meshullam traveled on to Genoa, marrying the daughter of a wealthy Portuguese Jewish banker. He went into business, was very successful, and the couple's first two children were born there. The names he gave his sons, Elijah and James—Elijah being the precursor of the Messiah, James the brother of Jesus—are suggestive of Meshullam's ambiguous religious identity, and it seems he was leading a double life. When he was discovered leaving a Christian service at the English consul's, his frantic father-in-law pressed him to deny it, upon which Meshullam disclosed his beliefs. Jewish feelings ran so fervently against him that he was forced to break up his business and flee to Leghorn in Tuscany, where he began again. His relentless father-in-law pursued him in an effort to take away his wife and sons; unable to persuade his daughter to abandon her husband, the older man exposed his son-in-law's apostasy, and Meshullam was forced to leave. The family went to Tunis, and he set himself up in business once more. By then Meshullam had made a decision about his sons' future, and he sent them to England, accompanied by the Christian missionary F. C. Ewald, who would later appear in Jerusalem as missionary to the Jews. When the Jews of Tunis learned that he had sent his sons to a Christian school, they hounded him, and he fled to Malta, hoping for the protection of the British government. Yet by then he had lost so much that he could not reestablish himself in business. Instead, he set himself up as a dyer, a trade to which his early travels had introduced him. (In doing so, Meshullam unwittingly embraced the profession of his forebears, dyeing having been an important craft among the Jews of Jerusalem in the twelfth century, as the Jewish traveler Benjamin of Tudela observed then.) On a trip to Malta in 1840, Meshullam met Samuel Gobat, who several years later would become Bishop of Jerusalem. Gobat baptized Meshullam and his wife.

Ill health, perhaps related to the toxic substances used in his trade, forced Meshullam to consider yet another move, and in 1841 he chose Jerusalem as his destination. Finding the city lacking in every comfort he was used to, and having received a token inheritance from his wife's father, he started an import business to furnish western residents with European goods. Immediately successful, he invested all his money in a huge shipment to be sent from London. The cargo arrived in Beirut, where his agent carelessly put it aboard open Arab boats bound for Jaffa. The boats foundered as they approached the shore, and everything was lost, probably stolen if not sunk. In despair and rage, Meshullam went to the coast, and returned an ill and broken man with little more to his name than two barrels of potatoes that had been salvaged. Meanwhile, a creditor had seized his store and sold its contents, leaving him destitute.

Meshullam's fortunes would slowly improve, and as he recovered, he was described as a striking figure—under five feet tall, yet possessing immense energy. He must have made quite an impression in those years. He was said to be a strange man who had journeyed through most of the globe in his youth, and from all accounts was filled with information gleaned from his wide travels. Next to his residence was a small piece of land, and as his health returned, Meshullam and his youngest son Peter planted the potatoes, which some travelers asserted were unknown in Palestine at the time. Agriculture was a novelty within the walls of Jerusalem, farming being largely concentrated in the Kidron Valley, where wheat and barley, figs, grapes, olives, pomegranates, mulberry, nut trees, occasional citrus, and artichoke thrived. Past attempts at raising vegetables for the hospital had failed, and as Mrs. Minor observed, no vegetables were grown within the city walls at the time of her visit, a few years after Meshullam's experiment. The success of Meshullam's potatoes was a momentous occasion, and it was followed by another fortuitous development. In the Easter season, the city was filled with pilgrims and visitors. Unable to find lodging, an Englishman was directed to Meshullam, who had for some time been assisting European travelers. Meshullam gave the visitor his house near the Damascus Gate and moved with his family into a small room. The grateful guest paid him well and encouraged him to open an inn, to which end he left his host all his traveling furniture. Thus the first hotel was opened in Jerusalem.

A few years later, in 1845, Meshullam was riding not far from Bethlehem, near the Pools of Solomon, so-named because of their association with the fountains of King Solomon and the Song of Songs. As with similar sites around Palestine, this site's identification was tenuous. Going back to Helena, mother of the emperor Constantine, Christian pilgrims and travelers to Palestine had endeavored to match the names of places mentioned in the Scriptures with actual locations. Helena herself was a most imaginative practitioner, paying little attention to geographical realities in her zeal to recreate Biblical days. Only as we near modern times does the method of identification change radically. By the nineteenth century, attempts at identification of Biblical sites, led by the American Biblical scholar Edward Robinson, were far more scientific, as the new field of Biblical geography took hold and acquired the scientific rigor of other branches of science. Both the medieval pilgrim and the nineteenth-century traveler, however, showed an interest in identifying not only those sites mentioned in the Bible's historical narratives, but also those named in the poetry and prophetic visions. When the scriptural literalist of the nineteenth century read in the Song of Songs: "A garden shut up is my sister, my bride / A spring shut up, a fountain sealed," he wanted to know where the garden and the sealed fountain were. It could not have been Jerusalem, where the Song of Songs is set, so he looked to the region of Bethlehem, already linked to Solomon's Pools. Nearby Artas, associated with events in the Bible's historical narrative and thought to be Etam, one of the towns that Solomon's son Rehoboam built to defend Judah, featured an underground fountain accessible only by a passage that was sealed with a large boulder. The conclusion was inescapable; the place must be the "fountain sealed." Indeed, the Arabic name, Artas, or Urtas in most travelers' narratives, is derived from the Latin *hortus clausus*, "enclosed garden." The significance of the site, on which a monastery was later constructed, was greatest for Christians, to whom the "sealed garden" of the Song of Songs was a reference to the "sealed" womb of Mary. The interpretation brought the circle of site identification to a close, offering a confirmation of events of the early Christian period.

When Meshullam came upon this rich valley, he was drawn

by the uncultivated yet attractive landscape with its fine old fig trees and wild pomegranates. Although the threat of Bedouin raids kept farming near the village of Artas to a minimum, Meshullam's imagination was stirred by the fertile Biblical associations. He followed up his visit by leasing (non-Muslims were not permitted to buy) a plot of land, a vineyard, and several wheat and grain fields. For the first few years, Meshullam ran his new farm from Jerusalem, but during the winter of 1849–50 he lived with his wife and children in a tent at Artas. He hired workers, whom he sheltered nearby, and built walls around the gardens. Soon he was raising vegetables for sale in Jerusalem. After a short time, Meshullam decided to leave the hotel and move his family permanently to Artas. He applied to the Pasha for permission to build a house, and upon approval, fashioned a four-room stone cottage at the lower end of the valley, using the hillside for the back wall, and rock outcrops to help form a stable and poultry house.

Meshullam was not the first European to move to Artas. Since the previous autumn, a young German employed by Meshullam had been living alone at the farm. The German thread in the story runs parallel to the American one; before long, the two would be intertwined. In 1846, one C. F. Spittler, from Basel, conceived of an idea by which he would spread a network of missionary stations throughout Asia and Africa, all emanating from Jerusalem, the great spiritual hub of his vast plan. To this end, he sent four young believers, all having taken a celibacy pledge, to Jerusalem between 1846 and 1848, where they lived in the newly established Brethren's House. In October of 1849, one of them, Henry Baldensperger, moved to Artas to work for Meshullam, and a few months later a second member of the German group joined him. Then the third moved in, and probably the fourth soon after. The Germans built stables for the cattle, and planted mulberry trees for a new silk industry with seeds sent from France. (It might be that

Solomon's Pools, near Artas. From *Picturesque Palestine, Sinai, and Egypt*, ed. Colonel Wilson, R.E., C.B., F.R.S., with numerous engravings on steel and wood from original drawings by Harry Fenn and J. D. Woodward (New York: D. Appleton and Co., 1883), vol. I, p. 145.

the Germans reintroduced the mulberry to Palestine, but as far back as the sixteenth century, a Spanish Jewish woman by the name of Dona Gracia had planted mulberry trees in Tiberias to begin a silk industry.) With a few more improvements, the Germans expected additional colonists from Wurtemburg and Alsace.

By that time the four young men had left the order and given up their vows of abstinence; there are references to one of the wives making butter, and to thriving children. They had apiaries in Bethlehem, and it was reported that they were responsible for introducing the art of beekeeping to Palestine. (Again, the verb used should be "reintroduced." Although the famous description of a land flowing with milk and honey, in Deuteronomy 8:8, referred to honey made from the date palm tree, there were actual apiaries in Palestine in the Talmudic period, between the second and fifth centuries.) There were also milking cows at Artas, and one can be sure that the milk and honey symbolism did not escape anyone. This enthusiasm notwithstanding, the German farm was short-lived; within two years, the group had left Artas, some attributing their departure to dissatisfaction, others simply acknowledging divergent aspirations. They did mention, however, that individuals from England, France, Germany, and Russia were similarly engaged—working to hasten the fulfillment of the prophecies —and "America does not lag behind." In fact, they reported in their letters, two "deputies" (no doubt Mrs. Minor and her companion) had come from America to investigate the prospects, and they proposed to return with twelve families "for the benefit of the Jews."

In February 1851, Meshullam wrote to Mrs. Minor conveying his pleasure at the news of her planned return to Artas. By that time, his harvest was considerable: carrots, beets, beans, cauliflower, cabbage, wheat, barley, oats, and finally potatoes, to which he must have had a sentimental attachment. Nonetheless, he lived in a precarious state. The physical labor was hard enough (one traveler observed that Meshullam's land, in a narrow glen between high, barren hills, was so rocky that it was hard to believe King Solomon had planned his pleasure gardens for there), but beyond the work itself were threats from the Bedouin who were accustomed to watering their flocks at the spring until Meshullam's arrival. In the early days they were resolved to expel him, and harassed him continuously, but he held his ground and eventually earned a degree of trust. By the spring of 1852 a traveler remarked that Meshullam was esteemed by his neighbors and was often relied on by the Bedouin when they had problems with the Turkish authorities—

a common predicament because the Turks were despotic and the Bedouin fiercely independent.

The pieces were falling into place; now all that remained was for Mrs. Minor to make her arduous way back to the little valley that would soon become the stage for an American-English drama of no small proportions. In April of 1851, nearly a year after they began gathering support, Mrs. Minor's son and colleague, Charles A. Minor, appealed in print to his coreligionists for further donations, referring to Meshullam's "cry from Jerusalem" for volunteers for their "Manual Labor School of Agriculture for the Jews in the Holy Land." Minor went on to say that in the past year cordial relations had developed between the American government and the Sublime Porte, and that the sultan of Turkey had issued a *firman* (a permit) to all denominations, which allowed them to build, own, and occupy lands in Palestine. In addition to the improved political climate, the harsh travel conditions which could not in the past be avoided were ameliorated by the establishment of a direct route between New York and Jaffa.

Charles Minor reported that, led by his mother, a small band of Sabbath-observing Christians not linked to any organized sect were at that moment ready to devote themselves to the work of teaching the Jews agriculture, if money could be raised for the voyage to Palestine and supplies provided to set them up in their new life. Among these supplies he listed tents, saddles, furniture, dry goods, and provisions, as well as more seeds, tools, and farm implements. Fundraising efforts must have been successful, for Clorinda Minor and her "small but picked band of enthusiasts" —herself and her son (whom she called by his middle name, Albert), Cyrus Thacher, Mr. and Mrs. Dwight and child, Lydia Schuler, and Emma Neil—set sail in early November, arriving in Palestine in March of 1852. Their arrival was hardly a noteworthy event, and was casually recorded nearly two weeks later by the British vice-consul in Jaffa. Three families of farmers and mechanics had arrived from the United States, he observed, adding that he heard they planned to settle down and practice agriculture. Two hundred more families were said to be following, but he could not attest to the accuracy of that report, which in fact was greatly exaggerated. Four days after the Americans landed in Jaffa, Meshullam's son Peter arrived to escort them to Artas. Although rumors were spread that twenty-five families had arrived, the group numbered a mere seven, not counting the baby. Heavy rains delayed their start, and they finally set out ten days later. An odd and singular caravan it must have been—sixteen camels loaded with 600 pounds each, eight mules, each laden with 300 pounds, including tents, furniture, tools, clothing, and medicine, and seven horses to convey the devout to the place of their calling. At sunset of their second day out they arrived in Bethlehem and were welcomed with tears of joy by their "beloved brother and sister Meshullam." In the next days, the members of the group who were in Palestine for the first time investigated the surroundings and pronounced them favorable beyond their already sanguine expectations.

Mrs. Minor noticed that Meshullam seemed to have accrued political power in the region. In Bethlehem he acted with more independence than two years before, and in general appeared to have gained influence with the Turkish authorities, the English residents of Jerusalem, and the local Bedouin sheikhs. On a visit to Jerusalem one day, Albert Minor was greeted by local Arabs who expressed the hope that more people like Meshullam would be sent to them, to which Mrs. Minor remarked forebodingly, "On this account there is much jealousy working among different parties here."

Yet there was little time for reflection or worry. Five months of washing begged to be attended to, gear had to be unpacked, and fruit trees nurtured. As soon as the rainy season was over they planned to pitch their tents and set to work, having brought with them whatever they could think of in order to introduce American agriculture to the Holy Land. By the end of the month, Mrs. Minor described looking out the door and seeing Meshullam, Albert, and the "other brethren," as well as an "Israelite" and an Arab planting potatoes. Several Jews from Jerusalem had already been there to ask about joining the effort, and others were waiting for the rains to pass. Longingly she wished for enough rooms to house them, having no doubt that many were ready to come. Meshullam concurred, insisting that only lack of money prevented them from accepting all the requests he had received.

❈

This then was the scene as the spring of 1852 came to the Holy Land. But such hopeful beginnings were not to find fulfillment in the reality at Artas, and some mystery will probably always be attached to the events of the following three years. Can clues to the dissension which developed be found in the early relationship between Clorinda Minor and John Meshullam? Was it inevitable that personal passions would override joint interests, or that religious and political issues beyond the scope of the settlement project would define the limits of commonality? Was the Holy Land too restricted a region to encompass all the intense energy that the various participants brought to it? We have bits of facts, pieces of correspondence, shreds of diaries. Perhaps a picture of this small yet tragic misalliance may be assembled.

Landing at Jaffa. From *Picturesque Palestine, Sinai, and Egypt,* ed. Colonel Wilson, R.E., C.B., F.R.S., with numerous engravings on steel and wood from original drawings by Harry Fenn and J. D. Woodward (New York: D. Appleton and Co., 1883), vol. 2, p. 128.

two

☾

The Battle for Artas

PERHAPS IT WAS too far beyond the limits of human enterprise for the strange union between John Meshullam and Clorinda Minor to have succeeded. Meshullam was an eccentric and independent loner; Mrs. Minor was the leader of a group that was untested physically, vastly underprepared for the realities of life in Palestine, and without a specific plan. They were driven by God-inspired zeal and were convinced that their mission would hasten the ultimate redemption, yet in their passion for God they may have overlooked human complexity. Further, and perhaps more crucial, the international stage that the Holy Land was becoming had grown crowded by their time, and it could have been that by 1852, when the Americans returned, their little drama was already subsumed in the monumental forces at work around them—without their having so much as an inkling. Were they all victims of power maneuvers taking place beyond their small farm? Were they pitted against one another as part of the struggle for dominance in the region? It would be mistaken to call them pawns, yet it might be essential to regard their independence as vastly more restricted than they knew, and to cast their fate in the light not of the divine plan that propelled them, but of the mortal exigencies that ruled the day.

❨

The story of what happened to Mrs. Minor and the others at Artas, constructed as it is from widely divergent versions of the events, is complicated, often hazy, and at times bewildering. So much detail has come down to us as innuendo that it is useful to keep in mind that there are relatively few incontestable facts. We know, quite simply, that in early 1853 an already long-simmering dispute between the Americans and Meshullam boiled over, the consequences of which were that their partnership was dissolved, the house at Artas seized, and Clorinda Minor's group evicted. Aligned with one or the other side were secondary antagonists including the dominating British consul, James Finn, his neophyte counterpart, American consul J. Horsford Smith in Beirut, and Smith's proxy, vice-consul Yacoub Murad, an Armenian resident of Jaffa. Everything surrounding the litigation that was precipitated by this quarrel is accusation, denunciation, and complaint. Such extreme discontinuity emerges that it might be wise to consider the comment of an observer in 1900 who cautioned that in most of the world arguments are two-sided, but in Palestine they are multifaceted.

In March 1852 the Minor party returned to Palestine and pitched their tents in the valley of Artas, just south of Bethlehem. For the time being, the scene was, if not idyllic, a model of cooperation. The Minor group was at work with Meshullam, joined by several Jews from Jerusalem, and the future looked promising. Mrs. Minor erected their large tent, twenty-two feet in diameter and eleven feet high, for a tabernacle and Sabbath worship, and

Approach to Bethlehem. From *A Home in the Holy Land, A Tale Illustrating Customs and Incidents in Modern Jerusalem,* by Mrs. Finn (New York: T. Y. Crowell, 1882), opposite p. 142.

the colony lived simply on bread and coffee or tea, molasses made from grapes, and occasional eggs, meat, and rice. By June they had plenty of fresh fruit—grapes, figs, pears, apples, pomegranates, and peaches—and by early fall they were harvesting a bountiful crop of sweet potatoes, which they had introduced to Palestine on their first visit. They were enjoying the climate and were bolstered by good health. Producing palatable flour was their main problem; theirs was very coarse, and working their mill taxed two men. Mrs. Minor exclaimed that a few barrels of American flour would be a great treasure until a new mill arrived. (The mill arrived two years later. A Bedouin sheikh who stopped at their new location for a visit was impressed by the ease of operation and the fineness of the flour ground by the Ross patent hand-mill, which Mrs. Minor had just received through the kindness of the inventor.)

The fertility of the region, the possibility of further land acquisition, and the cooperation of the local Arabs were factors that contributed to the pioneers' sense of optimism. They felt that Meshullam's influence was considerable and their safety thus assured.

The first outside view of the farm was offered by the well-regarded Dutch traveler C. W. M. Van de Velde, who happened to be visiting Palestine at just the time the Americans were arriving. Like most European travelers of that period, Van de Velde hoped to tour the shore of the Dead Sea, and he described how Meshullam arranged for the local Bedouin tribes to assist him. Coincidentally, Van de Velde had met the Americans when he was camping near Jerusalem just a few days earlier, so he felt he knew something about their mission, which he explained as being the fruit of a society that had been established in North America to send colonists to Palestine to join Meshullam's project. To gather funds, Meshullam's name had been "paraded in the Western world" at the head of subscription lists—this innocent observation, and Van de Velde's striking verb choice, perhaps suggesting that the Americans had used Meshullam's name rather cavalierly. Sufficient funds having been collected, the first seven settlers had arrived at Artas just a few days before Van de Velde himself, their camels laden with implements of all sorts. (Fifteen years later, an important Holy Land explorer erroneously attributed to Meshullam, rather than to the Americans, the introduction of the wheelbarrow, the first wheeled agricultural tool in Palestine since Roman days.)

Van de Velde reported their purpose to be both agricultural and missionary, yet although he thought them remarkable, he expressed certain reservations about the enterprise. What would the Americans do there? Would Meshullam give up his land to them? Would they be his servants? How would the newcomers get along with the Jews, to whom they wished to teach farming? These and more questions came to him as they all sat down to dinner. But Van de Velde had one overriding concern: Were the Americans trustworthy, or were they pursuing their own interests? If the latter, there would be trouble at Artas.

Another view of the settlement that was at odds with the general tenor conveyed by the participants' public pronouncements came from the highly respected American Biblical geographer, Edward A. Robinson. Just two months after the Americans arrived, Robinson, who was on his second trip to Palestine, visited Artas and met the Americans, whom he described as missionaries who wished to introduce agriculture to the Jews. (His comment, disparagingly echoed by Herman Melville a few years later, was that it was obviously visionary to think of converting the Jews into farmers.) But with no knowledge of the customs and language of the country, he went on, the Americans were helpless and were employed by John Meshullam, a converted Jew who formerly had kept a hotel in Jerusalem, and whose land had been yielding fruits and vegetables for the Jerusalem market for three years.

In an implausible observation, Robinson remarked that the Americans struck him as dissatisfied, and he claimed that they expressed a wish to leave as soon as they could support themselves. They told him they had brought American plows, but couldn't use them for lack of strong teams. Robinson did not elaborate on the state in which he found his countrymen, only adding that a colony of Germans who had been employed there two years earlier had also left. For Robinson this information was of only cursory interest, but his remarks are critical because of the discrepancy they locate at the heart of the Artas farm. If it were only a matter of the Minor group's having been there for a mere two months before dissension surfaced, it would be astonishing enough, for it is hard to believe that their disenchantment crystallized with barely a grace period. But it is not simply that. For the fact is that a week after Robinson's visit on May 14, the Americans entered into a contractual arrangement with Meshullam that legally and financially bound them to him. The contract, which they made retroactive to the first of April, stipulated that the Americans, who had come from the United States to work as "mutual assistants" of John Meshullam, had no claim on any of his possessions and agreed to meet half his expenses "from this day forward." They turned over to him one hundred pounds to be used to support the entire group. If any of that money, or subsequent contributions, was used on improvements or purchases, it would be done with mutual consent, and the Americans would be half-owners. The contract was signed by John Meshullam and his son Elijah, on one side, Charles A. Minor and Cyrus Thacher on the other, and two witnesses. The glaring absence of the signature of Consul James Finn suggests that something was not quite right. Either the two parties denied him an observer's role, which would have been foolish; or the consul withheld his signature—whether because he was opposed to the arrangement or because the Americans never produced authorization from their donors to enter into partnership with Meshullam. Whichever it was, one cannot help but wonder what could have possessed the Americans to enter into a legal relationship with someone toward whom they evidently showed public signs of disaffection after less than two months.

If relations at Artas fell apart as early as Robinson suggested, then either the deterioration was sudden, or Mrs. Minor, dependent as she was on donations, was concealing it from those at home. Shortly after her arrival, she wrote an enthusiastic letter to *The Sabbath Recorder*, the newspaper of the Seventh-Day Baptists, in which she detailed her activities. If Robinson's remark was accurate, then this sequence would indicate that between the writing and the printing of Mrs. Minor's letter, another, more sinister, reality had already emerged at the farm near Bethlehem. Yet whatever dark side there was, it simply does not show in the published correspondence. In letters written during the summer and even into the fall of 1852, Mrs. Minor gave an extensive picture of the farm in full operation, and the scene was hardly bleak. Their "family" of twenty-two was busily at work, the harvest was excellent, and twenty Jews "of the better class," who until recently had despised farming because of the Talmudic teaching that "the sons of the alien are to be their plowmen and vine-dressers," asked to learn farming. "This country and Jerusalem . . . [are] surely rising," she exclaimed, "and being built and cultivated." It was reported that the Baron de Rothschild planned to make a large purchase of land for agricultural reasons and would perhaps buy "the whole of Palestine," and one of their Jewish laborers reported that a remnant of the tribe of Zebulon, east of the Jordan, was ready to come and work for Meshullam because he was a Jew. Mrs. Minor declared that Arab sheikhs, rising up against the despotism of the Turks, were Meshullam's great friends; and while the pasha of Jerusalem did not dare leave the city walls because of the rebellion, they at Artas were at peace, with many Arab peasants coming to Meshullam for counsel. Their friend and mentor occupied a wonderful position, serving as "breakwater" between Turk and Arab and Jew. Even allowing for exaggeration (for example that the Chief Rabbi of Jerusalem came to praise their efforts), it is hard to deny that remarkable new developments were sweeping through the closed communities of Palestine.

Two important issues arise in connection with these early reports, one of which concerns the Jews' alleged aversion to agriculture. James Finn confirmed the desire of a growing number of

Plowing with oxen. From *Those Holy Fields: Palestine, illustrated by pen and pencil,*
by the Rev. Samuel Manning (London: The Religious Tract Society, 1874),
p. 17.

Jews to work the land, maintaining that among the Jews of
Jerusalem, particularly those of European descent, the "idea of
labouring in the open air for daily bread had taken root . . . the
hope of cultivating the desolate soil of their own promised land
was kindled." Contrary to what many supposed, it was not because of religious prohibitions that Jews had avoided cultivating

the earth, but for two other quite obvious reasons. One was security, which, as everyone knew, was impossible for Jews to take for granted, and for lack of which they generally remained within city walls. The other was that with no experience in farming, they were dependent on non-Jews for land, equipment, and instruction. Yet association with non-Jews, which in effect meant Christians, was fraught with ambiguity. When Finn noted the Jews' desire to earn their bread "from the ground, *the land of Israel,*" he mentioned their dissatisfaction at the "oppression of the Rabbis" who opposed these initiatives. The rabbis did discourage, even forbid, their congregations from working with Christians—but not because of an abhorrence of agriculture. Rather, it was the specter of conversion and the missionaries' unflagging pursuit of proselytes, as well as the threat they perceived to their Orthodox way of life.

Early in 1854, the seminal American Jewish figure, Isaac Leeser, editor of *The Occident, and American Jewish Advocate* and translator of the first American Jewish editions of the Bible and the complete traditional prayerbook, pointed out that enemies of the Jews—namely missionaries—had dared to insinuate that the rabbis forbade agricultural pursuits in order to maintain the people's dependence on charity. One missionary went so far as to say that as soon as an individual showed a disposition towards Christianity, he was "starved back into the ranks." Leeser took great exception to that analysis, pointing out that "the poverty of the Palestine Jews" had been taken serious advantage of by the powerful institution of the Church of England, with its formidable array of establishments—school, hospital, church—and "aided by a proselyte-hunting British consul," a reference to James Finn, an ardent missionary as well as a diplomat. In a series of highly charged articles, Leeser declared that "Israelites are unlabouring only when they are prohibited to toil at their pleasure, and *our* land is sterile only because the labourers are wanting to cultivate the soil." As proof, he cited the farm at Artas, where Jews were successfully tilling the ground under the direction of M——, who would remain unnamed, as he was an apostate. Leeser urged acceptance of assistance from Christians who wished to aid Jewish agricultural undertakings, saying, "we only war against false friendship, not against the persons of non-Israelites."

While there was something stirring within segments of the Jewish community that challenged domineering religious authority, the phrase "oppression of the rabbis" was a kind of standard missionary rationale which justified conversion attempts. It was very convenient for James Finn or Clorinda Minor or anyone else who had a stake in the matter to assert that the Jews were throwing off the shackles of the rabbis, the implication being that they were awakening to Christianity. But in fact it was largely a matter of being able to work without fear under Christian protection.

Ludwig Frankl, a Jewish visitor in Jerusalem around this time, was struck by what seemed to be a large number of Jewish converts to Anglicanism. Visiting the Anglican Church, he noticed the absence of any cross and the display of two marble tablets on which were inscribed the Ten Commandments. He found a Hebrew prayer book, and saw that it contained, along with "the usual ancient Jewish prayers," insertions pertaining to Christianity—all done so unobtrusively that "the neophyte is thus gradually habituated to the other faith." (*The Occident, and American Jewish Advocate*, commented on the Jerusalem church's practice of reading the service in Hebrew, "as though this perversion of the sacred language could entice the true Israelite from his devotion to his faith.") Frankl was pressed to account for a congregation of 130 baptized Jews, and concluded that those sheep being "brought within the fold by the shepherds" were no loss to the Jewish community.

While in East European communities Jews were always shocked by apostasy, the Jews of Jerusalem regarded it with indifference, either because they had grown accustomed to the frequency of the event, or because they "were quite willing to make a present of the proselytes, who . . . [were] . . . usually not remarkable for their high moral principle."

In a less sardonic tone, Frankl continued that if he could only close his eyes to the object of the mission, he should "readily admit that it has conferred many material advantages on the Jews," in the form of a hospital, a sewing school, a woodworking shop, and an agricultural project. But his cynicism prevailed as he looked at missionary work from the economic point of view, commenting "that these holy fishers of men use a golden net." It was no secret that many Jews went to Jerusalem for the express purpose of being baptized, because their baptism there was "attended with greater advantage to themselves." Many families of converts quickly became reconciled to the change, for the family ties were not loosened, and in most cases they knew that inwardly the individual maintained his Jewish convictions. Frankl himself had heard family members say, "'He will soon come back, after he has helped himself.'"

Other travelers regarded the missionary endeavor as frustrating and bound to fail and suggested that the Jews were especially hard to indoctrinate because the two religions were so different in what they professed. Hunger was the greatest incentive to conversion, for the poverty of the Jews of Jerusalem was greatly aggravated by sharp price increases. People were starving, and oil, wheat, and bread, their chief staples, could not be obtained.

The religious ingredient was inevitably stirred into the mix that was Artas. Mrs. Minor believed that her group was the envy of competing interests who had tried unsuccessfully to persuade

View of the English church and attached consulate. From *Stirring Times, or Records from Jerusalem Consular Chronicles of 1853–1856*, by the late James Finn, M.R.A.S., edited and compiled by his widow (London: C. Kegan Paul & Co., 1878), vol. 2, frontispiece.

Meshullam to join them before the Americans returned. The Russian-backed Greek Orthodox Church, with its great financial resources, were their "greatest opposers," offering bribes and engaging in intrigue to get Meshullam to relinquish Artas to them. The English Episcopal Mission, backed by Consul Finn, was trying to tempt Meshullam to send away the "poor Americans" and join them instead. Mrs. Minor had no doubt that if Meshullam did switch his allegiance, money would "come in loads from England," and she did not know how long they would be able to hold on, for keeping that "most favorable spot in Judea" was very expensive. Acknowledging the receipt first of $421, then of $71, she was obviously soliciting more.

Yet notwithstanding Mrs. Minor's continued paean, it becomes clear that the prevailing mood at Artas changed drastically and relations began to disintegrate after only a short time. Though it would take two years for the conflict to extend to the highest levels of the American and British governments, local consular intervention was called for from the very beginning. Two of the primary actors in the imbroglio were the American consul in Beirut, J. Horsford Smith, backing the Americans, and James Finn supporting John Meshullam, a British subject.

Finn is somewhat enigmatic. He was a man with a powerful will, unwavering convictions, and the authority to act on them during his long tenure as consul from 1846 until his removal from office in 1863. He had a significant effect on the welfare of the Jews of Palestine, acting as their self-appointed protector. Though his philo-Semitism was defined by his commitment to converting the Jews, and his consularship was marked by missionary activity, it is also clear from consular records that Finn, along with his wife, was deeply affected by the deteriorating condition of the Jewish community in the mid-1850s: "We became aware, as we had never before been aware, that there is among the Jews of Jerusalem an amount of misery and hopeless poverty, inconceivable to those who have not been eye-witnesses." Finn also initiated significant employment efforts on their behalf that were not contingent on their receptivity to missionary efforts. Indeed, at one point he angered the missionaries of the London Society by refusing them access to one of the sites where Jews were employed, realizing they would have pressed their cause during the afternoon break for prayers. Finn defended his obstruction; if he had allowed the missionaries onto the site, "it might have savoured of attempting to convert needy people by taking advantage of their distress."

One of Finn's early programs entailed sending prospective Anglican converts from Jerusalem to work at Artas. Four such men were employed in 1852, when Mrs. Minor arrived, and it seems that Finn should have been favorably disposed to the Americans, regarding them as reinforcements for a project that was perfectly consistent with his own goals. One could imagine that Meshullam, a convert farming the land and trying to draw other Jews by his example, might have been the paradigm which Finn strove to replicate in large numbers. Yet all of this was apparently not the case, and one of the mysteries that remains as part of the Artas story has to do with what motivated Finn—what he wanted for himself personally, what for his God, what for his nation, and what for the Jews, with regard to whom only a cynic would insist he wanted only their souls.

In that crucial spring and summer of 1852, when the Meshullam-Minor project at Artas, if not the scene of one happy family, was nonetheless in full operation, further pressures were being brought to bear on the farm, and the level of stress was increasing rapidly. At issue was the rather unpredictable Ottoman taxation system. An aqueduct which ran from the Pools of Solomon to Bethlehem and Jerusalem had been maintained by the villagers of Artas since Suleiman's time in the sixteenth century, in exchange for tax-exemption. That centuries-old arrangement was suspended in October of 1850, and suddenly the villagers as well as Meshullam felt abnormal financial urgency. Meshullam was greatly relieved when the Americans came to throw in their lot with him; one of the very first things he did was take them up to Jerusalem both to meet Consul Finn and to pay the taxes on Artas.

Finn meanwhile wrote to the pasha asking him to reconsider the wisdom of a policy whereby reclaimed land was not only taxed, but taxed retroactive to the time Meshullam began farming. The Turkish authorities had already sent cavalry to Artas demanding taxes, whereupon the villagers had fled in fear. But though a large sum was paid by Meshullam and his friends, soldiers occupied the village and demanded more. In early summer Finn requested guidance from his superiors in Constantinople, asking that an annual figure be settled on. Referring to raids by Bedouin in which sheep were stolen and fruit trees destroyed, Finn inquired what the valley's residents were getting for their tax money, if not protection of their possessions. The following year, Finn was still acting on behalf of Meshullam and the peasants of Artas, forwarding to the Sublime Porte a list of their grievances stemming from the taxation issue. And yet another year later he complained once again that increased taxes might be borne if security was guaranteed. Meshullam had taught the villagers of Artas cultivation, but their corn had been destroyed by jealous residents of another village, and the Taamari Bedouin (the tribe that lived in the region) were permitting their cattle to break down fences and trample the gardens. Some of the hostility was assuaged by an arrangement dividing water rights, but the agreement was not being honored by all tribes.

Finn maintained hope for the Artas farm. When he asked his government to persuade the Sublime Porte to relent on the taxation issue, he added that "the farming enterprise of Mr. Meshullam has excited a considerable degree of interest among benevolent persons in various countries." Claiming that his interference at Artas was required by this matter, he was clearly anxious to rid the valley of the discomfort caused by indeterminate taxes. Maybe he also wanted to eliminate the American presence, which was, at the least, an embarrassment to him, as he indicated when he reported that the pasha wanted to know who the original lease-holder was, and who were "the strangers consisting of sickly men and unmarried women living on public alms, who had no official representative nearer than Beyroot able to speak their language."

It hardly sounds from this sequence of events as if Finn was Meshullam's nemesis, yet the Americans claimed that such had been the case since Finn's arrival in Jerusalem in 1846. In the days when Meshullam was still an innkeeper, Finn was so hostile that he refused to forward reservation requests to Meshullam and went so far as to intercept travelers on the road, bringing them to his own residence rather than let them go to Meshullam's hotel. Mrs. Minor's son Albert claimed that he had often heard Meshullam call Finn "Mr. Cheat," and that at one time, probably in the spring of 1851, relations had become so bad that Meshullam was forced to request assistance from Finn's immediate superior, the British Consul General in Beirut. While this Colonel Rose was riding to the rescue, Mrs. Finn, in tears, begged Meshullam and his wife to forgive her husband. Finn resumed his alleged aggression after Rose left Jerusalem, and a year later, Meshullam was desperate enough to consider appealing to a consulate other than his own. One hardly knows what to make of these charges. It is unlikely that they were wholly contrived, yet no real substantiation can be found. Relations between Meshullam and Finn would eventually plunge into enmity, but that would not be for another decade. If there was animosity between the two men at this early point, it was not widely advertised.

Finn visited Artas occasionally while the Americans were living there. One spring evening around this time he called Meshullam aside and discussed with him his opposition to the American project and to Meshullam's part in it. Albert Minor claimed that Meshullam warned them that Finn's jealousy and power were so great that they had better hope for the early appointment of an American consul in Jerusalem, or Finn would persuade his government to expel them. This was probably the moment at which the Minor group, circumventing the American consul in Beirut, directly petitioned the United States Senate to appoint Meshullam as the American vice-consul for Jerusalem, though it is not clear if they requested the appointment for Meshullam himself or for one of his sons. In either case, their action had an edge of calculation to it, but if they were promoting young Meshullam, the incident meshes with a strange, otherwise mysterious, accusation that would be made against them more than half a century later. Finn's wife Elizabeth, an active partner in her husband's affairs both diplomatic and missionary, claimed that the Americans had persuaded the reluctant Meshullam to join them by flattering him and claiming they could get his eldest son made a consul. The episode is not without the possibility of intrigue. Was Meshullam pulling the strings that would result in the fulfillment of his own ambition, or was Finn as conniving as Meshullam made him out to be? Did Albert Minor exaggerate Finn's competitive instinct in order to embellish his later complaint to Washington? Or was it true that Finn had bribed an Arab sheikh to deny the Americans an opportunity to secure farmland, and that Finn himself planned to buy a piece of land where the Americans already had planted wheat and barley? Was this a transparent case of personal greed?

One might also ask what the various parties had to gain by their obstinacy. Palestine was not America in mid-century, where any small dispute could be resolved by one party moving a few inches west on the map, or out of earshot of the next fellow's ax. In Ottoman Palestine movement was hardly possible for reasons of safety and permissibility, and unforgettably, the very life of every western settler was defined by this one particular slice of geography, the hallowed land they had all come to redeem. It seems so obvious that the Americans and British had somehow to join forces in order to succeed that one wonders how they missed the point. Did their roles—the ones they assigned each other as well as the ones they assumed for themselves—define the contours of their relationship and determine the outcome from the very onset? Was failure written into their labor because competition for political visibility meant that lines were being drawn at the very moment they needed to be crossed? Ironically, the diplomatic network that might have saved the Americans became their undoing; if their cause was inadequately served, it was because there was no one capable of serving it.

Since 1839, when Great Britain became the first western nation to establish an official presence in Jerusalem, the British consulate had offered assistance to non-British residents of Jerusalem. To an extent, they needed a population to defend in order to justify their presence, and since there was not yet a Protestant community, the consulate offered protection to stateless Jews. The policy was well suited to the interlocked goals of the British missionary and diplomatic vanguard, and was equally important to the Jews. Without the umbrella of the British government, for example, Jews would not have had the confidence to venture for work outside the city walls. Extending diplomatic protection to resident Jews was a complex issue and underwent constant reevaluation, but with the other beneficiaries of the British consulate's services, non-British travelers, the situation was simpler, involving plain diplomatic hospitality rather than long-term responsibility. When it came to American citizens in Jerusalem, it was natural for the English consul to see to their interests and safety, and there were numerous cases of American travelers—including Lt. William F. Lynch, the naval officer who had conducted the century's major research effort at the Dead Sea just a few years before Mrs. Minor arrived—receiving assistance from Finn. But the circumstances that would find Mrs. Minor and her group in distress obviously closed off this avenue of aid, Finn being at the very heart of their predicament. In the absence of Jerusalem representation, J. Horsford Smith, the American consul in Beirut, became the necessary protector of American interests in the Holy City, and it was to him that their appeal was addressed. The problem was that in an emergency, the distance between Jerusalem and Beirut precluded an effective response, and for this reason, the United States, like Britain and Prussia, employed a system of vice-consularships throughout the Ottoman Empire, by which a non-American resident was authorized to serve the needs of American citizens. Such was the case in Damascus, Aleppo, and Jaffa, for example. But remarkably, given Jerusalem's attraction for travelers, the United States had thus far failed to appoint a vice-consul there.

When the U.S. Senate did not act on Mrs. Minor's request in 1852 to appoint Meshullam vice-consul, the group wrote pleadingly to J. Horsford Smith in Beirut. In response, Smith designated an Armenian businessman named Yacoub Murad, who had been serving as both American and Prussian vice-consul in Jaffa. This rather routine appointment provided for a sequence—at times a comedy—of exchanges between Smith and Finn that reveals as much about the two consuls as all the rest of their correspondence put together. Unfortunately, the comedy was lost in the disproportionate consequences it engendered, and events of the next few years were shaped as much by the personality conflict between the two men as by the substance of the dispute between Clorinda Minor and John Meshullam. Against all reason, the appointment of an American vice-consul to whom Finn strenuously objected threatened the stability of Anglo-American relations in Palestine at a time when the approaching Crimean War was already bringing turbulence to the region. Furthermore, in exposing incompetence on the part of an American diplomat, the incident highlighted the inadequacy of the American quasi-presence in the region.

The drama over the vice-consular appointment began innocently enough, in late April 1852, when Smith, responding to the

Jerusalem, Via Dolorosa. From *Landscape Illustrations of the Bible, consisting of views of the most remarkable places mentioned in the Old and New Testaments, from original sketches taken on the spot.* Engraved by W. and E. Finden with descriptions by the Rev. Thomas Hartwell Horne, B.D. (London: John Murray, 1836), vol. 2, plate 9.

Americans' request for diplomatic representation, took the necessary official steps with the United States legation in Constantinople to acquire a *firman* to legitimate the appointment of Murad. Smith then traveled to Jaffa to accompany his new vice-consul to Jerusalem, where he presented him to the pasha. There were several foreign consuls in Jerusalem at the time, Prussian, French, and Austrian, as well as English, and they all, including Finn, called on Smith and Murad. When Smith and Murad returned Finn's visit a few days later, however, they were stunned by the English consul's refusal to receive Murad. Smith was deeply insulted, both professionally and personally, and expressed his anger to Finn. Finn sent a cordial response, explaining that he did not receive Murad for reasons which he would put in writing, and asserting that he would only deal with Murad through a lesser official. "Jerusalem is a peculiar place," Finn patronized, advising Smith that consuls need to be high-quality individuals.

Smith replied that their aborted meeting removed the friendliness he had felt for Finn, who had no right to behave so rudely during an official visit, ignoring Smith's outstretched hand and declaring that he could not receive him accompanied by "that man." Finn replied patiently, saying he thought they had parted on good terms. Anyway, he went on, it was not an official visit; Smith was simply returning the social call that the Finns had made two days before. As proof, Finn recalled that Smith had apologized for the absence of his wife. Finn explained that Smith had caught him by surprise, only telling him on Thursday that he had appointed Murad to the post, and Finn had had no opportunity to make his objections known. Thus when Smith arrived at his home, he was abrupt because he wanted to prevent Smith from making an official introduction.

In response, Smith asked in effect what Finn was talking about.

Of course Finn's visit had been an official one—how could it have been otherwise when the two men didn't even know each other? And if it *wasn't* official, how dare Finn *not* make an official call, as all the other consuls did. New to the business of diplomacy, Smith was unschooled in the shades of meaning that defined diplomatic contacts, and from the beginning, his lack of experience, exacerbated no doubt by Finn's intractability, was an impediment to progress on any front. His letters have a whining ring to them, while Finn's notes sound patient and conciliatory. Call it what you wish, Finn wrote back; he would be willing to regard it in any light that expressed his friendship for Smith and his government, if only Smith "had not laid so much stress upon it." About his refusal to receive Murad, Finn expressed the hope that Smith "will cease to think that the honor of the United States' nation and government is at all implicated in this course."

All the fuss was certainly an annoyance, but the repercussions for the American settlement at Artas would be catastrophic. The explanation Finn offered for his behavior was that Yacoub Murad, who had changed his name from Yacoub Serapion, had been accused of "serious crimes of public notoriety," and that the charges had never been fully investigated. Murad, or Serapion, had been the secretary of the U.S. vice-consul at Jaffa, one Murad Aroutin, in whose high esteem he was held. On Aroutin's death, Serapion was appointed to his mentor's position, and was asked by Aroutin's widow to settle her husband's estate, care for her in her last years, and assume the name Murad. All of this took place around 1850, and Finn, claiming he did not know of any name change, reportedly had no qualms about addressing Murad in his new position as vice-consul at Jaffa. Two years later, just when the American group requested Smith's protection, Murad, who had become one of the wealthiest men in Palestine by virtue of his inheritance, was accused of defrauding the widow Aroutin's foster children of their share of the estate.

The charge of fraud, Smith insisted, was supported only by the Finns and a few others who had personal stakes in the matter. One of the "few others" was an Englishman who had lived nine months in Syria and who coveted the vice-consularship. In his disappointment, this accuser, writing out of "zeal for the honor of the United States Government," went so far as to publish an anonymous letter in American newspapers, in April of 1852, in which he spoke of Murad as "a notorious plunderer of orphans," and, perhaps implying necrophilia, claimed Murad "treated the dead body of his late mistress in a manner, which, if . . . true, would show him to be an inhuman monster." Smith passed on the contents of the letter to some prominent Americans in Jerusalem, in response to which they wrote to the Senate, condemning the letter as "a tissue of miserable calumnies," and attesting to the character of Murad, whom they had known for ten years.

What Finn's antipathy was really about, according to Smith in his counterattack, was nothing but a loan that Finn had requested from Murad in June 1850, and which the latter, doubting Finn's ability to repay it, had refused. Smith charged that Finn was in the habit of borrowing money from whomever he could and had run up a huge debt that his salary couldn't possibly cover. This, and nothing else, he contended, was what the colossal mess was all about.

Finn's finances were a perpetual source of anxiety to himself and his family during his tenure in Jerusalem. While it is true that over the sixteen years of his service, Finn's debt would grow to an unmanageable size and contribute to his dismissal from office, his impoverishment was not the result of careless folly. He was eager to increase his land holdings at several locations in Palestine, including Artas, and he had grand plans for various employment projects for the Jews of Palestine, to which he evidently applied all his loans. He never used his holdings or his influence to enrich himself; on the contrary, he was often destitute, his own house lacking heat in winter. When an official investigator arrived from London to examine the morass, he was quite sympathetic and offered moral, if not practical, vindication. For one thing, both the cost of living and the income tax had gone up in Jerusalem without a commensurate raise in Finn's salary, and the consular allowance was altogether inadequate, especially given the increase in ceremonial expenses because of all the consuls and patriarchs then residing in Jerusalem. True, Finn had overextended himself with the land purchases that contributed to his debt, and his financial judgment was clearly flawed. But those purchases, "if not exclusively prompted by . . . schemes of benevolence towards the Jews . . . [were] closely associated with such designs." The investigator, one Lord Francis Napier, then turned and chastised Smith, who had been desperate for the consular post in Beirut because it was a sound job. Napier commented that Smith, who took the post to promote his own commercial interests, "might have learned in his own undeserved, but repeated, notorious, and unredeemed misfortunes in trade to exercise a greater charity in laying bare the embarassments [*sic*] of another."

Finn strenuously denied that the refusal of a loan had anything to do with his professional conduct, and he accused Murad of hiding behind the aegis of the vice-consularship to avoid answering the charges against him. Finn's government, however, chastised him on this count; he had no business refusing to recognize Murad, as it was not his place to investigate Murad's character. What came out of this, on the positive side, was a moment of rare concurrence between the two adversarial consuls. Finn advised that the large number of American citizens traveling in Palestine warranted "a United States gentleman of some standing in his own country" to serve their needs. Smith, bitter at the insult he perceived to himself and his nation, arrived at the same conclusion, expressing the hope that one day only Americans would represent Americans abroad, so they would not have to suffer the abuse of foreign consuls.

Finn comes across as an exceedingly principled man, sometimes excessively so, even sanctimonious, but he insisted that his "habits of life have never been those of rudeness and brutality." He seems to have been matched against a novice who cast himself as some David against Goliath. Smith's letter to his government, cataloguing the grievances both he and the Minor group had against Finn, was characterized by the British investigator as a list of unsubstantiated accusations marked by "excitement." True, remarked Lord Napier, Finn had a temper and was not without blame, but he was not the evil persecutor that Smith claimed. Smith had exaggerated, unconsciously or with malice, because his own "temper was embittered by many circumstances which combined to overcloud the latter period of his residence in Syria."

On a personal level, Smith warrants sympathy; as one of the early representatives of a diplomatic corps that was not even a professional body at the time, he was tossed into a situation that literally had no precedent. Yet one of the differences between the two consuls was that Finn, who also had no formal diplomatic training, knew Arabic and Hebrew, and this in itself may be an indication of a more serious approach to the post. A number of observers of affairs in the Ottoman Empire throughout the first two-thirds of the nineteenth century commented on the lack of professionalism among American foreign service representatives. They lacked training, and they did not serve long enough to make use of the experience they gained. Personally, they were often of mediocre quality, and professionally, they behaved like the novices they were. Smith was a businessman who hoped the appointment would help him in commerce, and though he was not unique in that respect, nor necessarily unfit for the position, he seems to have reacted immaturely in stressful conditions. Unfortunately, the ramifications of Smith's demeanor extended well beyond the personal arena. His excessive national sensitivity and misplaced pride were part of a developing fiasco by which the United States missed an opportunity to project a respected image in a region where long-held power had largely crumbled, and a new configuration was already presaged.

When Smith declared that Finn's removal from office would be a cause for rejoicing, he was speaking from a very myopic point of view. Finn had many items to his credit, and though he may not have been on good terms with everyone, he did manage to perform an impressive balancing act. As far as his devotion to the region's various populations was concerned, Finn was unsurpassed. He made frequent trips to locales where violence had erupted, whether between Christian factions, or between Muslims and Christians, or when Jews were persecuted, and there were instances when only his intercession prevented bloodshed and murder. In short, Finn was obviously more than the nominal protector of western and minority interests in his domain. To lose him might have given personal satisfaction to Smith and the Clorinda Minor colony, but his dismissal would have left a gap of influence at a very sensitive time for all westerners.

The Murad affair escalated until Smith went back to Beirut, intent on ignoring those comments of Finn's that seemed to be "intended as ridicule." He asked that Finn simply send him an official report detailing the charges against Murad, to which Finn replied wearily (if the deteriorating legibility of his normally careful handwriting is an indication) that Smith should just take the private letter with all the details and mark it official. That should have been the end of the matter, but Smith would not let it go. Two weeks later he wrote from Beirut in a rage that Finn wouldn't comply with his demand to deliver the complaint in official form. Further, it was not Finn's prerogative to refuse to receive Murad, he fairly screamed through his pen. Finn, relying on standard diplomatic phrasing to stave off yet another round of hostilities, replied simply that he had the honor of receiving Smith's correspondence and referred him to the communication which he formerly had the honor to send him.

With this there is a lull in the battle. Could it be that those brief weeks, when the relationship between two key figures was set in stone, had already determined the fate of the Artas project, removing any possibility of flexibility and turning a resolvable dispute into a diplomatic crisis? The Minor group, whatever their eventual culpability, had arrived at a most unpropitious moment. By early 1852, enough ire between the English and American diplomats had already been spread to fuel far more than their one small conflagration. These events, which should have been nothing more than an unfortunate prelude to the American arrival, assumed a centrality out of proportion to their intrinsic meaning.

That the agricultural and diplomatic branches of early American and British activity in Palestine were intertwined is not a surprise given that they were both grafted to the same stock, the religious meaning of the Holy Land for Protestant Europe and the United States. At the heart of the matter for Clorinda Minor and James Finn, though not for J. Horsford Smith, who was an unwitting participant in their drama of divine expectations, were the souls of the Jews of Palestine. With such a nebulous prize in the offing, it was perhaps inevitable that the contest between Clorinda Minor and James Finn would become a clash of wills and imagination. That clash would coalesce around an innocently composed document.

The Americans claimed that, guided by their example, Jews were coming in large numbers and asking for employment. On being turned away for lack of funds, a group of Jews proposed submitting a petition for publication in the United States as a means of raising money for additional land and equipment. In June the petitioners' representatives delivered the document, with sixty-three signatures. Referring to Artas and Meshullam, they wrote: "And we, the poor sheep, came to the benevolent . . . [Meshullam] . . . with bitter hearts—for our souls are bowed to the dust—and we said unto him, 'How didst thou come to this?' and he answered us, saying, 'Ye are as I am; if ye will labor in the ground as I do this day, then shall you also eat of her fruit, and be satisfied from her goodness; for he that tilleth his land shall be satisfied with bread.' When we heard this we greatly rejoiced." They hoped that contributors "may show mercy, truth, and great righteousness unto us and our households, our children and little ones, that we may be enabled to buy land, make us gardens and vineyards, and labor in the ground; that we may walk in the ways of our forefathers, and be fed from the labor of our own hands . . . and the land that shall be bought by the help of God (blessed be his name) shall be unto us and our children for an everlasting inheritance."

The various versions of what happened next are so at odds with one another as to stymie reason. Meshullam passed on the Hebrew petition to Albert Minor, who took it to Finn for translation. (Why Finn was needed is not clear, since no doubt Meshullam knew Hebrew.) Finn promised to bring it back when he and his wife dined at Artas the following week, in time to make the next mail. The Americans later claimed that not only did Finn fail to return the petition, but after dinner, he informed them that he was beginning an investigation into their affairs. He questioned them aggressively about the nature of their relations with Meshullam, and when Minor referred to their contract, Finn reportedly sneered, asking how they could suppose it to be valid without his approval. When he demanded they turn over their accounts, they complied in part, though they considered it a gross overstepping of his authority. Meshullam felt vindicated, telling the Americans that Finn's actions proved he had every intention of sabotaging their project. Minor again requested the petition, Finn kept delaying; finally it was too late for it to be posted. What had made the mail, however, was a copy of the document, attached to which was a note from Finn, intended for "wide publication" in the States, appealing to the American public for financial assistance to employ Jews at Artas—with *himself* and two other appointees designated to oversee all affairs there. The Minor group, Finn wrote, had consented to this arrangement.

The Americans were spared another social call from Finn for some time, but Meshullam, who had regular meetings with him in Jerusalem, kept the group apprised of developments. He reported that Finn and "his English friends" had made "advantageous offers" to him if he would break his contract with the Minor group and enter into partnership with them instead. Finn tried to tempt Meshullam by persuading him that with Finn's name attached to the project, large sums of money could be raised in America and England. Meshullam assured Mrs. Minor that he had rebuffed the overtures; he would not betray those who had first befriended him, even if, as Finn promised, all the Americans' expenses were repaid and they were sent home "well satisfied."

Aspirations to integrity may not be so easily fulfilled. The Americans noticed signs of irritation in Meshullam, and he began complaining about his large expenses and uncertain income. Finally he admitted that Finn's offers of security had weakened his resolve, and he began equivocating. Caught in a moral bind, Meshullam made an appointment with Finn, broke it, made another, delayed again. Finally Meshullam, apostate again, turned over to Finn the Artas records, even submitting some "base fabrications" against the Americans as the motivation for his conduct. Perhaps his dilemma required him to invent a rationale for his treason; or perhaps he was demonstrating that the neophyte could be counted on for zealotry.

Before long the Americans received notice to appear at the British consulate with letters and papers, advising them that failure to do so was punishable. Hoping to reach a civil agreement, they reported to Jerusalem, accompanied by a new friend, Dr. James Barclay, the only American missionary in Jerusalem. (Barclay, one of Finn's partners in the projected expansion of Artas, was probably ignorant of the conflict of interest.) The group offered information, shared correspondence, answered questions, but to no useful purpose; Finn's inquiries were crass, his manner imperious, his objections unreasonable. He contested the amount of money the group had received from home, though the specific amount was recorded in their account books and certified by Meshullam's own signature. It made no difference that Meshullam had even sent receipts to the United States. It was a hopeless quagmire.

Yet this sequence of events was subject to quite a different representation, as Finn's own account shows. As Finn contemplated the possibilities suggested by the petition, he saw a chance to enlarge the project and went down to Artas to talk it over with Meshullam and the Americans. He told them that certain individuals in Jerusalem expressed a desire to help, and he suggested a committee of three, including himself and Dr. Barclay, to oversee the expansion. The proposal was well received by Meshullam, who agreed to place himself "under an efficient working superintendence" of like-minded people. Meshullam was evidently the only one who liked the idea, and the Americans warned him to "take care how you put yourself under an organization, you lose your liberty." But Finn, whether with innocent zeal or disingenuously, claimed the whole group was favorably disposed to the plan. He hastened back to Jerusalem, drew up an agreement, and sent it to Artas for approval. No reply was forthcoming, and Finn again eagerly drew his own conclusions, taking the silence of the "friendly Americans" for assent. To the United States, England, and Germany he sent notice that donations would be received for "promoting agriculture in Artas by Jews for their own relief and sustenance—keeping strictly and singly to that point alone on the basis of the freest religious toleration."

Finn declared that once the terms were agreed upon, forty Jewish families were prepared to go immediately to Artas, and ten rabbis promised to send their own sons. Yet the vow to disclaim missionary intentions was evidently not widely trusted by the rabbis in Jerusalem, who, according to Finn, tried to dissuade Jews from joining and promised that Montefiore and Rothschild would give them vineyards. Pressure was added, Finn said, and the Jews were forbidden to participate unless they had a synagogue in the valley and brought down a *shochet* (ritual slaughterer), and unless Finn gave his word not to try to convert them. Expressing distress at seeing heads of families in a "state of bondage," Finn promised. His correspondence shows vitality and excitement at being able to act on behalf of the petitioners. It does not reveal a conscious attempt to sabotage the Artas project; he sounds, quite simply, carried away.

Yet what was the prize that the valley near Bethlehem had to offer? Was it financial gain? political power? personal glory? If so, why come, in 1852, to the little village of Artas, an isolated corner of the struggling Ottoman Empire, to pursue those vanities? Something else, far less palpable, was at work, and it persisted unmitigated in the imaginations of those whose lives became increasingly defined by the project.

Indeed one feels much the same about Finn as about the Americans—that the very motivation he attributed to Meshullam was probably a projection of his own aspirations. The Americans and Finn concurred, at least at first, about Meshullam's character. As Mrs. Minor had, Finn lavished praise on Meshullam, who always cared about "the poverty and degradation of the Jewish people," and practiced "hospitality and charity to his nation." Meshullam had been known to carry sacks of produce to Jerusalem's Jewish Quarter, where he sold them well below regular prices, and it was a common occurrence for entire Jewish families to come to Artas for a quantity of grain, a bag of vegetables, or just a good meal. But though Meshullam wanted to do something even more substantial to help the Jews, it is doubtful that he ever entertained grandiose ideas. Rather, he was an unwitting magnet for other people's dreams, and his farm triggered bold schemes of salvation in the minds of both Clorinda Minor and James Finn. They seized on the petition, with its implications for the dramatic realization of their dreams, as the supreme legitimization of their respective causes. But though the document meshed perfectly with their ultimate goals, it seems fundamentally to have had nothing to do with Meshullam's own modest labor.

Finn's motivation is complicated. In the world that he knew, a western nation's missionary presence in the Ottoman Empire was virtually a prerequisite for political power, and he might have been taking precautions by discouraging American competition.

Valley of Urtas, or Artas. From *Picturesque Palestine, Sinai and Egypt*, ed. Colonel Wilson, R.E., C.B., F.R.S., with numerous engravings on steel and wood from original drawings by Harry Fenn and J. D. Woodward (New York: D. Appleton and Co., 1883), vol. 1, p. 140.

Yet this does not take into account his great passion both to assist and convert the Jews. That in itself might have been so powerful a force that he could not abide any perceived intrusion on his turf. His intention in the valley may indeed have been subversive, but his behavior in these years of 1852 to 1854 should be read in the context of his full ambitions, which were not by any means simply self-aggrandizing. Finn may have been initially propelled by envy of the Americans' potential for success at Artas, but after the petition was made known to him, the farm assumed a new urgency. Obviously his version of events is radically at odds with the Americans'. When the document was brought to him, he was struck by the implications it had for the work he was already involved in—both creating work for Jews and exerting religious influence. Probably this was a momentous event for him, a moment when all his material strivings on their behalf, as well as his inchoate yearnings to do something vast and permanent, were suddenly offered the chance of fulfillment.

The Americans, on the other hand, undoubtedly contributed to the web of misunderstanding. Their intentions were vague, and as far as Meshullam could fathom it, Mrs. Minor's ardor had expanded into an unrecognizable obsession. Imagine the unsuspecting Meshullam, his worldly adventures behind him, as a simple farmer. Mrs. Minor's arrival must have been like a visitation—the strange woman from abroad, accompanied by her "brother," offering him partnership, in what it was not clear. Finn explained the essence of the difficulties at Artas as being caused by "a couple of fanatics or worse," who came from the United States and stayed at Meshullam's hotel, where they heard of his "romantic adventures." They wrote them down from memory when they got home and printed a pamphlet. Proclaiming him to be an "intensely religious man" working for the restoration of the Jews, they appointed themselves his agents and set themselves up to collect funds for the "wonderful enterprise." Only later, after "Miss Adams" returned as Mrs. Minor, accompanied by her twenty-year-old son and "some young women," did Meshullam perceive their duplicity. Did Mrs. Minor ever have a clear idea of how to accomplish her goals before the petition provided a focus?

The petition dispute, it could be said, was the essence of the battle for possession of the meaning of Artas. Questions that one might ask, if posed out of the larger context, are virtually irrelevant: What went wrong so soon between the Americans and Meshullam that they would vilify each other even as their work was getting under way? How could they have so grossly misread one another's intentions? Who was to blame for the breakdown in relations? Those questions frame only part of the picture, for in a sense, Meshullam is a distraction. The real struggle was not between John Meshullam and Clorinda Minor; it was between Mrs. Minor and James Finn, between two contradictory visions, and their embodiment in two uncompromising and passionate individuals.

❦

As if the Artas partnership weren't under relentless siege already by an invisible but all too palpable array of forces, there was yet more ammunition to boost the enemy arsenal. One round took the shape of a citizenship dispute involving an Englishwoman named Mary K. Williams, who had not come with Mrs. Minor from the United States but had joined the group two months later, in the fateful month of June 1852. In the middle of June, Mrs. Minor took Lydia Schuler and Emma Neil, the two young women who had come with her from the States, on a sightseeing excursion to Jerusalem. They stopped to see the house in which Mrs. Minor had stayed during her 1849 trip and bumped into the elderly Miss Williams, who had just arrived from England. Their coincidental meeting delighted Mrs. Minor, and within a week, Miss Williams was settled at Artas. Meshullam, however, had not invited her, and did not welcome her. Rather, he asked Finn to come down and "ascertain the exact intentions of Mrs. Minor's party." Finn ordered the elderly woman to leave, but she put herself under his protection, claiming British citizenship. When he demanded proof, she placed herself under U.S. protection, saying she was a naturalized citizen, and notifying J. Horsford Smith to that effect. The business dragged on through the following year, with Finn objecting that Miss Williams could not renounce Britain and be granted American citizenship while in a third country. Smith gloated as he prepared to strike a blow to Finn's national pride, asserting that everyone needed diplomatic protection, and furthermore, that Miss Williams had lived in the United States for seventeen years, with only five required for naturalization. Finn was triply galled. He claimed that the five-year period did not apply in Turkey; that she could not renounce her allegiance to the Crown; and that she didn't need protection anyway. Eventually he took the matter to his superiors and was instructed to relent.

The expansion of the community necessitated new housing, but even something so mundane was wrapped in ambiguities. When the Americans arrived at Artas, Meshullam made arrangements for the construction of three rooms over his house. Mrs. Minor was thrilled at the construction, comparing it to Jerusalem, where the whole city was "building . . . outside the city walls, as never before." Yet suddenly, Finn sent an "official command" to Meshullam forbidding him to enlarge Artas without his consent, since he was the superintendent. With the rainy season approaching, this was an especially "cruel and illegal measure" according to the Americans. Forfeiting the summer building months, Meshullam finally started construction in the autumn, and his colleagues suffered in their tents until the rooms were completed around Christmas. Even as their new home was taking shape, however, the American group was shrinking. Albert Minor, frail and ill, left suddenly in November and went back to the United States, depriving the group of one of its two male members and leaving his mother increasingly vulnerable, especially given the male-orientation of the environment.

Utter deterioration followed. In December, with the new house nearing completion, the Americans complained that their erstwhile colleague, Meshullam, had been absent from Artas for some time, though it was the planting season. They let Meshullam know that for their part they were willing to continue the partnership, but that if he wished, they would agree to dissolve it "in an amicable and Christian manner." Two weeks later they received his reply: yes, he wanted to dissolve it, since the Americans had not performed as they promised and had caused him great financial loss. To bolster Meshullam's accusation, Finn sent a statement to the United States claiming that the Americans had impoverished the formerly prosperous Meshullam. If Meshullam needed further support, he received it from an impartial source, a traveler who happened by that winter. The visitor was at first impressed with the Americans, but by the end of 1852 was greatly disappointed. He had hoped they would bring industry and piety to their enterprise, but there seemed not to be a worker among them except a mechanic named Dwight ("Mr. and Mrs. Dwight and child" were original members of the Minor group), who had been expelled after a quarrel.

The two consuls engaged in attack and counterattack, the substance of which would soon move to the public arena in the form of reports to Washington and London. Finn went first, describing Meshullam as having lived quietly, "enjoying the works of his own hands," until the Americans came and "worked themselves into a connection with him." Only after a period of time were Meshullam's eyes opened to the "trickery with which he had been duped." Unfortunately, as Finn later pointed out, the purpose of promoting agriculture among the Jews had been lost sight of, for reasons he delineated. The members of the Minor group were totally ignorant of agriculture, they kept the seventh day as the Sabbath, and they knew no language other than English. Soon after their arrival, Meshullam's family was divided, the children "disobedient to their parents and siding with the Americans," at the instigation, Finn intimated, of Miss Williams, who had arrived "in an artful manner" and was responsible for much of the "evil" at the farm.

Finn's campaign was suspended by his illness and recuperation in Jaffa, and the Americans preempted him by submitting their own list of grievances, including the accusation that Finn was intercepting their mail. Meshullam's eldest son Elijah had become the Americans' ally, and he told them that his father had opened a letter at Finn's direction and had spent some of their joint funds to repay a debt. Mrs. Minor claimed Finn had instructed the postmaster to deliver all Artas-bound mail to him so he could have full control by collecting all donations sent from the United States. Finn, on the other hand, said Meshullam had complained to him that Mrs. Minor was opening mail directed to Meshullam, Minor, & Co. and withholding the contents, though Meshullam was the senior partner. Thus he authorized Finn to intercept business correspondence in order to match contributions against expenses. Finn acknowledged he had done so, on the grounds that Meshullam was "the principal partner in the Firm if such a term can be applied without ridicule to the kind of association which existed at Artas."

What especially provoked Finn was Smith's automatic acceptance of the Americans' charges, Smith's defense being that he was not at liberty, "in the absence of more definite evidence," to question the truth of Mrs. Minor's claims. Finn invoked his record of friendliness to United States citizens "of high character" and found it mind-boggling that "as soon as these persons now in Artas, whose immoralities are being denounced throughout the United States, merely write to you a charge against me of oppression and persecution . . . you take it for granted as true." The accusation of immorality which Finn cited would swirl around the Artas affair for the next few years, never fully articulated, never put to rest. Finn instructed Smith that "the moral character of Mrs. Minor has been severely censured in the United States in public prints, but some revelation will, I am informed, be published of a nature unexpected even to you." Although the allegation may have had to do with the manner in which funds were raised, it is more likely that Mrs. Minor's decision to travel, in the guise of a sibling, with a man neither her brother nor her husband was the undoing of her reputation.

By the end of January 1853 the Americans were desperate. The missionary Dr. Barclay, in whose Jerusalem home some of the group had taken shelter, described their "sad predicament," and Clorinda Minor herself sent urgent notes to Beirut begging Smith "for God's sake," to come to their aid. At the end of the month, Smith set out. Arriving at the beginning of February, he described the Americans as filled with fear of Meshullam and Finn, the latter of whom they believed was trying to drive them out in order to gain possession of the valley for himself. Smith announced that Finn should choose a meeting place other than the British consulate, since it was there he had been insulted the year before. Finn denied he had insulted him, but he suggested the Chancery. Smith had a penchant for trying to get the last word; yes, he had been insulted, and no, his memory was not at fault, he replied.

The two consuls got down to the business of opening the books so accounts could be settled and the separation legalized, but it was not to be easy. Meshullam claimed the Americans owed him money, that in addition to his own resources, his son's wages had been donated to the cause. Mrs. Minor rejoined that Meshullam was nearly penniless when they arrived, and that he was "living upon them, and the contributions of their friends in America." Those contributions, however, had been made, if not *to* Meshullam, then *because* of him; a mass of material—letters, pamphlets, newspaper articles, poetry, dreams, and visions—from the United States all attested to the fact that Meshullam was recognized as the founder of the Artas project. The truth was, Finn admitted, that the two parties had been useful to one another, the financial resources coming primarily from the States, and Meshullam providing "a salubrious and fruitful locality," not easy to come by in Palestine.

The Americans, deriding Meshullam for charging them for dead horses and broken crockery, laid claim not only to half the house and half the implements, but also to half the vegetables in the ground, half the seeds and wood, half the poultry and half the mule, half the peach trees and bed of horseradish, half of ten jars of wine, damages for lost planting time, and compensation for corn and vegetables taken by Meshullam when he left in December. In Mrs. Minor's view, Meshullam had abandoned Artas and thereby abrogated the contract; to Finn, he had been forced out, and he too was in desperate circumstances. Unable to return to Artas, he was reduced to renting a house in Jerusalem and, accustomed "to the free air of a country life . . . [was] pining in the unwholesome city." Worse, he had believed the Americans came to do good for the Jewish people, but they had done nothing except "vilely traduce" his character. The only exceptions were Mr. and Mrs. Phillip Dickson, a young American couple who had arrived in late 1852 as representatives of the American Agricultural Mission, and who lived and worked at Artas, though not part of Mrs. Minor's group.

Much of the legal altercation stemmed not from the aborted contract between Meshullam and the Americans, but from a document drawn up and signed by the two consuls themselves. After Smith arrived from Beirut in early February 1853, Finn and Smith agreed to the dissolution of the partnership. The two men settled on a division of the tools and crops, but could find no Solomonic solution to the problem of the lone mule, which was to be a major point of contention for the next two years. The house was the most complicated issue. Both Mrs. Minor and Meshullam were so assured of being awarded full possession that they had forfeited the right to half, referring the matter to the donors in the United States whose contributions had made construction possible. All this was validated in an official document signed by Smith and Finn and dated February 11, 1853. Bearing the official seals of the two consuls, it confirms that Meshullam, Mrs. Minor, Charles Albert Minor, and Cyrus Thacher had been engaged in agriculture at Artas "for the purpose of benefiting the Jews," and "that the entire company, have been sustained and supported, by the private funds of the said C.A. Minor." It further states "that from the contributions of Citizens of the U. States, a substantial house has been built, at Artas"; and that in the light of difficulties between the concerned parties, which resulted in their separation, it had been agreed by the two consuls and the contestants "to refer the question of final and entire ownership of said house, to the decision of the contributors and donors of funds, in the U. States." Until word came from the States, the house was to be vacated and "sealed or nailed up" by Smith or his representative, and the keys deposited at the U.S. vice-consulate. The two consuls signed the agreement, though for some reason the concerned parties themselves did not, and Smith returned to Beirut. Within a day Finn realized he had made a mistake, and he wrote to Smith that he could agree to the house's being locked, but not "sealed up, nor nailed, nor screwed," because English money had helped build it. Needless to say, Smith rejected Finn's reasoning and condemned his timing.

Given the vitriol between the two men, the plain issues had become clouded; and between the two consuls, as someone observed, "such a feeling had grown up that no question, which demanded the exercise of patience and forbearance could possibly prosper in their hands." Arbiters were appointed in April, but they made no headway, and by June everyone was frustrated, not least because Charles Albert Minor, the principal person signing on the American side, had been in the United States for seven or eight months.

No departure date had been set by the two consuls, but the Americans were expected to vacate Artas. At the end of February, Finn wrote in Italian to the U.S. vice-consular representative in Jerusalem, who happened to be the younger brother of the Jaffa vice-consul Murad, over whom Finn and Smith had come to blows. Finn objected that rather than pack up, the Americans had brought some baggage back from Jerusalem and had done further planting. Finn demanded that Murad evict them, and Murad refused; he took his orders only from Smith. Outraged, Finn responded that obviously Murad didn't understand Italian, so he would try again in English, and Murad had better get the note translated since he intended to go to Artas the next day.

As he had threatened, Finn went to Artas to notify the group, by then nearly all women, that they would have to pay rent if they remained. Hearing he was on his way, they locked themselves in. They had planted a new crop of sweet potatoes, and they announced their intention of remaining until everything in the ground was ripe. Unable to gain entry to the house, Finn went to Meshullam's rooms below, where acting vice-consul Murad soon arrived. Finn and Murad argued about which nation owned the house, and finally the group evacuated one room, over which Finn's aide placed British seals. The feisty Miss Williams tore one down and, according to Finn, took a stick and hit his assistant. Demanding that she be held responsible, he wondered if her change of national allegiance weren't a convenient means of escaping retribution. "It appears that not law but violence prevails among the U.S. Citizens at Artas," he judged.

Finn tried a different tack, announcing that the sheikh who had been appointed to guard the group had notified the pasha that he could not defend women who were without a protector, especially at that time, in the midst of a drought, when more than the usual number of "wild Arabs" were coming to the valley for water. After more angry correspondence, Mrs. Minor began packing in mid-March, digging up their winter crop of potatoes, beets, and carrots, and loading camels with furniture and tents. She was particularly incensed because no quarter was given Miss Schuler, who was sick at the time. Further, they were denied bread, though they had already paid for the wheat; and third, Meshullam would not allow the use of any animals, including the disputed mule, to help transfer their belongings. The demoralized group traipsed up out of the valley and moved to a house that Dr. Barclay provided for them in Jerusalem. So they left, one year, nearly to the day, after their arrival, and the American presence at Artas came to an end.

No sooner had they arrived in Jerusalem than a letter was delivered from Finn's office, signed by Meshullam, in which the Minor group was assailed not with regard to legal matters but to character. It was, they interpreted, an expression of the opposition's frustration at their failure to defeat them utterly. The group began disposing of items they could not transport, and undertook preparations to return to America. When Finn heard they were about to leave the country, he insisted they be held until the accounts were settled, but Smith refused to order their detention.

Within a few weeks the Meshullam family was back at Artas, presumably in their own downstairs apartment. Only the locked doors of the contested rooms and the American seal posted on the window hinted at the drastic transformation that had come over the farm in the last year. So matters stood when a reply came from the United States regarding ownership of the house. Once again, the facts do not lend themselves to obvious interpretation. The initial correspondence makes no distinct reference to ownership; rather, the various donors simply verified that they had given certain sums of money, totaling around two thousand dollars. Smith jumped on the figures, declaring it to be nearly the entire amount that had been spent on the three rooms, and exulted in this apparent proof of American possession. Finn of course disputed Smith's reading of the contributions.

Their bickering continued into early summer, when a further statement arrived from the States, and Smith triumphantly announced the question resolved. He sent Finn a letter from *The Presbyterian*, a Philadelphia newspaper, in which the editors recounted how they had become interested in Artas through Mrs. Minor, and because they considered it a largely American enterprise, they recommended it through their columns. They said money and supplies had been donated not to any individual, but to an organization, the Agricultural and Manual Labor School in Palestine. Contributions were received through the J. L. Boyd Agency (Boyd being Mrs. Minor's early traveling companion) from November 1851 through February 1853, and any money or goods still en route should be directed towards the Americans "now associated for agricultural purposes in Judea, wherever their locations may be." Another letter stated that the group had been supported by C. A. Minor, and that Meshullam provided valuable services. The house was built with money from the United States, and because of the estrangement of the Minor group from Meshullam, the American donors awarded it to the American party. Should they sell the house, the proceeds would go to their enterprise, as would any future donations. Thus the matter seemed concluded. Yet there was still another twist in this convoluted sequence, for

View in Jerusalem, near St. Stephen's Gate. *Landscape Illustrations of the Bible, consisting of views of the most remarkable places mentioned in the Old and New Testaments, from original sketches taken on the spot.* Engraved by W. and E. Finden with descriptions by the Rev. Thomas Hartwell Horne, B.D. (London: John Murray, 1836), vol. 2, plate 38.

it seems that assigning the house to the Americans was not the prerogative of the American donors, no matter what the finances indicated.

Finn acknowledged receipt of the correspondence in mid-June, adding rather devilishly that he recognized the right of Minor and Thacher to sell half the house to Meshullam. Smith was incensed: what do you mean, *half* the house? By the end of the year there was another hitch. Finn refused to allow Meshullam to make an offer, because Smith had neglected to return certain crucial documents he had borrowed from Finn and which were "of great importance" to their case. Finn asked repeatedly to have them back, and Smith, after delaying, promised to "send for" them, saying, "I have no papers in my hands such as you mention . . . and if I had, I should pay little attention to such a 'demand.'" Exasperated by Smith's carelessness, Finn wrote for advice to his superior in Constantinople, asking that this intractable issue be put to the U.S. legation there. Finn asserted that in sending an extract from the wrong letter, Smith showed his ineptitude and "how much he . . . is liable to be duped by his Clients residing in Jerusalem."

As outraged as Smith was by what he took to be Finn's continuous manipulations, the outside investigator, Lord Napier, took the unsettled accounts to be ample reason for delaying sale of the house. For one thing, Meshullam had no money, and only if the accounts were settled in his favor would he be able to buy the rooms. If the house were sold to someone else, what assurance did Meshullam have that he would be reimbursed, since Albert Minor had long since gone back to the States, and Cyrus Thacher was about to leave? Still, Smith insisted that Meshullam had been given enough time to make an offer, and the house would be put up for general sale on the Americans' behalf. Finn countered by declaring invalid the document signed by himself and Smith in February. Smith returned that if Finn was waiting for further instructions from his superiors in Constantinople, he would put the whole case before Washington.

In addressing himself to the U.S. Secretary of State William Marcy in 1854, Smith wished to make it known at the highest level that Finn had violated the word of the British government in forsaking the February 11 agreement, which bore his seal. Smith begged that attention be paid to the matter of Finn's persecutions of the Americans, who could no longer reside in Jerusalem or its environs due to his oppression. Time after time Smith had sought to settle the accounts, and Finn had refused. "No despot exercises more authority," he asserted, than did Finn in his self-created little kingdom. Finn's co-conspirator, as it were, was his wife, Elizabeth

Finn, whom Smith characterized as a meddler. Smith stated that no American could look forward to living peacefully in Jerusalem as long as Finn retained his appointment. He excused the British legation at Constantinople as being too busy with political affairs to look into the charges he leveled against Finn; thus he sought the help of his own government and hoped for "early action, to obtain redress for unprovoked insults and wrongs." Included in his packet to the State Department was a statement from Albert Minor and Cyrus Thacher, detailing their version of events. They were all too eager to offer a history of James Finn's "illegal, and oppressive course towards . . . American Citizens." Charging Finn with "aggressive and determined opposition," the writers insisted they had arrived in Palestine as neutral parties, politically and ec-clesiastically, and had been well received by everyone—Christians, Muslims, and Jews—except James Finn.

The year 1854 provided the encore, as if the performance needed one. Having convinced himself that the house was American territory, Smith sent an American citizen, a missionary by the name of Jones who had just arrived in Jaffa, to take possession of the building in the names of Minor and Thacher. Meshullam had allowed a lodger to enter one of the rooms through a window. Jones kicked him out and "installed a slave Abdallah," then went up to Jerusalem. When Finn learned of it, he had Abdallah turned out, put iron plates over the keyholes, and placed British seals over the doors. Jones got wind of it and went back, reportedly bran-dishing a seven-barreled revolver or pistol (which Smith denied) and threatening to beat Finn's aide. He tore off the plates and seals, locked two rooms, reinstated Abdallah in the third, and left. Abdallah fled soon after. Before long, Finn gave Meshullam per-mission to occupy the whole house, a distinct violation of the fifty-fifty arrangement.

The British government responded to the American grievances

that had been forwarded by Washington to James Buchanan, head of the U.S. legation in London, by sending Lord Francis Napier in the spring of 1855 to hack through the thicket of charges. Surprisingly, Napier's report was a fundamental vindication of Finn's actions with regard to the Americans. His opinion was that Finn bore responsibility for minor things and might also be reprimanded for signing, then annulling, the critical February 1853 document too hastily. But in fact the document was altogether illegitimate from the start. Though it bore the seals of the two consuls, it stipulated that the "parties concerned" agreed to the terms. Yet neither Meshullam nor Minor had ever signed it—meaning that the document never had legal validity and was in effect a nullification of itself. Second, the decision from the United States regarding the house did not, in spite of the evidence presented, emphatically award the rooms to the Americans, not by any means. Napier apparently put little stock in the letter from the newspaper editors, and confined himself to a close examination of the figures, asking which donations were earmarked for the house, and which for the general enterprise. The sum given for the dwelling had to constitute more than fifty percent of the total in order to prove American ownership, yet Napier himself felt the results were ambiguous, at best, and may even have indicated the opposite of Smith's conclusion. In fact, Napier impugned Smith's integrity, or at least his credibility, suggesting that the American consul had been somewhat less than scrupulous in studying the list of contributions, and had practiced an exaggerated process of selection in choosing what to submit to Washington.

But all this was minor compared to the final point. The fact was that neither Meshullam nor Mrs. Minor—nor even both of them together—had ever owned the house—and even if they had, they did not own the land under it. In 1849, Meshullam had leased the land for five years, his contract specifying that at the expiration of the term, ownership of all structures would revert to the landowners. The agreement between Smith and Finn could hardly be called a binding contract if it had no legitimacy under Turkish law. Before the two men put the issue to their respective governments, Finn had written to Smith explaining he hadn't realized that Meshullam's lease nullified their agreement. He cautioned Smith that if Meshullam were to be forced out, the peasants would have a right to the house and could call on their government to demand that Smith remove the Americans—upon which the house would be theirs, "despite any papers signed between you and me."

Lord Napier asked for clarification from the Ottoman authorities: If English subjects and American citizens had jointly built a house on land without securing possession of the soil, who owned the house? Could the English/American party get a title and sell it? The answer that came back to them was laced with contingencies, since a labyrinthine procedure would have to be followed in order to unite the land and the house. But the essence of the reply was that value had to be assessed separately, and the owner of the more valuable, whether land or house, had to buy the other piece. Finn and the new American consul in Beirut, Henry Wood, who had just arrived to replace Smith, were instructed to use their "ingenuity" to find a way to resolve the problem. The two men, who to everyone's relief were on good terms, had agreed to lock the house and deposit the keys with Wood in Beirut, place the U.S. seal over it, and give the accounts of Meshullam, Minor, & Co. to arbitration. Lord Napier described Finn as open and gracious, and Wood as so conciliatory that Napier wished he had been empowered not just to inquire but also to offer a solution. Meshullam, incidentally, was to pay for half the mule plus two years' interest, that stubborn problem finally being resolved.

When Meshullam asked for Finn's assistance in prolonging his lease to the farmland at Artas, he presented his own case for the first time. Through him there was order in the valley and the people were able to pay their taxes. Meshullam taught the peasants to grow European vegetables, reclaimed land, and largely prevented raids by Taamari Bedouin. What he got in return was subsistence for his family. The absence of any reference to the Jewish aspect of the Artas project is noteworthy, and it seems that the lofty interpretation of the scheme may have been largely an American invention. It is true that way back in 1851, when Mrs. Minor was planning her return, Meshullam was seized by enthusiasm and wrote that he could "never shrink from a purpose now become *my duty*," and that he was animated by the thought that one goal united him and her. One senses, however, that he was temporarily enthused, and that for him the divine motivation was uninspired. Indeed, at the same time that he was embracing Mrs. Minor's goal, he expressed misgivings about how he was represented abroad for fundraising purposes: It would be "deleteriously unjust" to attract "romancers or speculators, bearing little likeness to what I acknowledge myself to be—*a laborer for my brethren's fellowship and encouragement*, which position only accords with yours and my united design." In her zeal, Mrs. Minor may have filled his head with fantasies of what he could do for his suffering people. In this sense, one has to consider the possibility that Mrs. Minor used Meshullam— used his name to gather funds, used his farm to establish her base, but more than that, used his work to substantiate her vision. Not with malice, not with conscious cunning, but out of a passionate need to fulfill her spiritual longings, thwarted as they had been in the United States, she replaced reality with an imagined version of what Meshullam was doing at Artas. For only then could her desire be justified, and her faith given form. She was accused of trickery, flattery, lying, and cheating. But maybe it was at the core a matter of self-delusion which should invite from a distance of time not scorn but pity for how much energy was consumed. Clorinda Minor would soon finish her life while attempting again to translate her vision into reality.

A contemporary observer recorded his suspicions about "pure" missionary efforts, suggesting that one had to ask if the glory of God or oneself was at the heart of the matter. If personal glory were Mrs. Minor's goal, it might have been inevitable that an end would quickly come to this singular American dream. But an obsession with mortal renown does not mesh with the very real image of American settlers pushing up their sleeves and digging their hands into the soil of Palestine. Further, glory was more immediately attainable through conventional missionary work than through hard physical labor. Missionary work offered the possibility of large numbers of converts to hold up to an admiring public back home; this other work—preparing the land for the Second Coming—was a logistical headache of monumental proportions. Beyond that, an outsider noted as the project was falling to pieces, the trouble at Artas arose precisely from the fact that Mrs. Minor was not a real missionary, and the next phase of the story hinges on that very observation. Driven Clorinda Minor was, but she was not mad, and she had one last chance to realize her dream of farming in Palestine.

Part II: Jaffa

☽

. . . O mountains of Israel, ye shall shoot forth your
branches, and yield your fruit to My people Israel; for they
are at hand to come. For, behold, I am for you, and I will
turn unto you, and ye shall be tilled and sown.

Ezekiel 36:8–9 (translation from Soncino Books of the Bible,
London: The Soncino Press, 1950*)*

three

☾

The Move to Jaffa

THE AMOUNT OF energy that was squandered in the dispute at Artas cannot be calculated, and one can only guess how many years and even lives might have been saved, and how much might have been achieved, without the strain of such a debilitating and protracted struggle. Yet despite the transience of the Artas enterprise and the fragility of the project that would follow, Clorinda Minor's work was a stone thrown into the pond, casting circles of ever greater circumference. Although her impact cannot be precisely measured of course, the American group was one of the catalysts to emerging Zionist sentiment among the Jews of Europe. Jewish-sponsored agricultural projects took root a decade later, and some of the earliest Zionists, taking the American farm as their paradigm, encouraged Jews to look to their inheritance in Palestine.

There is no record of what Mrs. Minor thought about during the two months of her retreat to Jerusalem in March 1853. Despite James Finn's decree that the Americans not leave the country until the accounts were settled and their supposed debt to Meshullam paid, Cyrus Thacher left after the group's eviction from Artas, leaving Mrs. Minor as the only senior member of a group that consisted entirely of women. Everything pointed to a necessary abandonment of the project. But that didn't happen. It seems Mrs. Minor became acquainted with a European landowner by the name of David Clossen, a German Christian who had recently bought an estate near Jaffa "to do good for Israel." Bold or foolhardy depending on one's angle of vision, Mrs. Minor leased his land and moved to the coast. Soon she would be joined by a new corps of Americans. The project they began would have a good deal more solidity than the one at Artas, and a significance that would reverberate well into this century.

☾

The move to Jaffa was a stroke of luck for the Americans. Removed from the isolation of Artas, they found themselves near a developing center of activity on the southern coast of Palestine. While in the past travelers from abroad disembarked at Beirut and made their way south, as Mrs. Minor herself had done on her first trip, recent changes eliminated that leg of the journey. Steamships had begun service, and in the 1850s Jaffa was starting to be included in the regular shipping routes from both Europe and the United States. Some observers, such as the American missionary Dr. Barclay, saw such developments as part of the divine plan. Steamship lines, the planned railroad, the coming of the telegraph to Jerusalem, the Crimean War—what could it all mean if not that God had major plans for the Land of Israel? Jaffa, described as a "close and filthy town," was in a lovely setting looking out onto the sea and surrounded by dozens of estates or "gardens," *biarrahs* in Arabic, that were watered by large pools. "Whilst the citron, orange, lemon, banana, and palm strongly impress upon those

Jaffa from the sea. From *Landscape Illustrations of the Bible, consisting of views of the most remarkable places mentioned in the Old and New Testaments, from original sketches taken on the spot.* Engraved by W. and E. Finden with descriptions by the Rev. Thomas Hartwell Horne, B.D. (London: John Murray, 1836), vol. 1, plate 89.

gardens the peculiar features of tropical scenery," wrote Barclay, "the appearance of the apple, pear, quince, Indian corn, and sweet potatoes seemed almost to carry me 'back to old Virginny.'"

Mrs. Minor did not languish in Jerusalem, for within two months, in May 1853, she had rented the Jaffa garden. By July she, the two young women, Miss Schuler and Miss Neill, and the elderly Miss Williams were living in a large stone house with spacious rooms and wide terraces. There was not a pane of glass in all its thirty-three windows, she mentioned in order to emphasize that in spite of talk of war with Russia, she felt as safe as in her cottage in West Philadelphia—more secure, in fact, than in the States, "where we were liable, within the safest bolts, to have the midnight robber take not only our light valuables, but our life also, and where we were never, as here, secure from the alarm and danger of fire."

They employed Jewish laborers, who resided with them, and the house was filled with the Jews' many guests. At any given time fifteen people slept there. Mrs. Minor claimed she had the general sympathy of the Jews of Jerusalem and Jaffa because of her recent "persecutions and trials," and because the Jews believed that her regard for them was untainted by missionary motives. Her presence was important because "freedom and protection in the country are new things to them."

Americans had never before resided in Jaffa, and her small group was attracting friendly interest. Everyone was cordial, and both Jews and Arabs requested medicine, which she was glad to offer. The Arabs were afflicted by inflamed eyes, and she wrote to the States asking if anyone could recommend a remedy. The Jews were destitute and needed clothing, which Mrs. Minor's Presbyterian friends were sending for winter. But above all, the Jews entreated her for employment, and Mrs. Minor bemoaned her state, asking where was the Christian help she so badly needed. "Oh that God would arouse his people to feel for this long degraded, oppressed race, whose debtors they are." She was worried that when the Jews returned from "their great autumnal feast" (Sukkot, the festival of Tabernacles) in Jerusalem, she would not be able to employ them any longer.

For the moment, however, she warmed to her new life, grateful for good health and enjoying a simple and pleasant routine. They went out to the fields at daybreak, rested in the heat of the day, and resumed work until after sunset. A German family, a Lutheran missionary and his wife and her two brothers, who had left Germany in 1848, lived nearby and farmed "for trade." Mrs.

Minor described them as poor, but good workers, and they had learned Arabic quickly. One of the young men, John Grossstein-beck, had come to live with Mrs. Minor; he was her protégé, and she his surrogate mother. Before long he dropped the prefix from his surname, creating the family name of the American writer John Steinbeck, whose grandfather he was.

They gathered first fruits in midsummer, and the harvest continued into October. The cotton was five feet high and covered with pods; they had corn, potatoes, lima beans, eggplants, tomatoes, and beets. Even their "American" crops—Indian corn and sweet potatoes—were thriving. Only the beans planted in the hottest months had failed, but Mrs. Minor was confident that in another year they would "better understand their season," especially as they were learning to irrigate. They did have one technical problem. The summer crops needed watering, and drawing a sufficient amount from the well was laborious and expensive. Mrs. Minor yearned for the "simple Yankee chain-pump" that was due to arrive in the spring. If it worked, she knew she could sell hundreds "at a fair price" to Arab farmers who faced the same problem of summer irrigation. Only the expense of the "machinery" then in use—that is, the feeding and caring for mules—prevented widespread agriculture from becoming a reality. "What a benevolent work would it be, to bring water within the reach of the industrious poor—now only enjoyed by the rich," she wrote to her son.

When Mrs. Minor arrived in Jaffa, she found a congregation of seventy families, mostly of North African origin, led by Rabbi Raphael Yehuda Menachem Ha-Levi. Rabbi Ha-Levi had come to Jerusalem from Dubrovnik, and was sent by the Jerusalem Rabbinate to oversee religious affairs in Jaffa twenty years earlier. He must have been a most vigorous man, for he was seventy-five when Mrs. Minor met him, and she described him as being highly esteemed by both Turks and Christians. He himself owned a garden comprising over five thousand trees—citrus, pomegranate, mulberry, almond, apple, apricot—which he had planted over the years. He visited Mrs. Minor regularly, and he and his family stayed with her when the heat in town was severe and one of his ten children was ill. Mrs. Minor wrote that they celebrated their first Sabbath evening together, and she described their delightful situation overlooking orange groves and the blue sea. Writing to her son, she expressed love for her "devoted child" who had suffered so greatly at Artas and sacrificed so much for this work.

To a large extent, Mrs. Minor's success would depend on the receptivity of the Jewish population to a project linked with deeply committed Christians. The Jewish perception that tucked behind Christian offers of assistance were motives of a different order might have been reason to reject her overtures. The problem in 1853, with the outbreak of the Crimean War and Russia's ban on charity to Palestine, was that deprivation was turning into starvation, while at the same time more elderly Jews were arriving from Europe to live out their days in the Jewish holy cities. In a very immediate way, Jews had no choice but to risk contact with Christian groups, and the Clorinda Minor colony offered them the chance to learn how to save themselves. The Jews of Jaffa were especially responsive to Mrs. Minor because Jaffa was not one of the four holy cities and therefore received comparatively little of the *chalukah* fund. Mrs. Minor argued, and in this her feelings were shared by others, Jews and Gentiles, that the Jews of Palestine were condemned to a system of "hereditary pauperism" that was aggravated, not relieved, by the charitable contributions of both Christians and Jews, because charity alleviated the immediate hardship but did not address the root of the problem, a profound lack of employment. In recalling her decision to emigrate to Palestine, she said that the "degenerating tendency" of idleness and need over

בעז"ת

לקראת שרי ורוזני היושבים בער"י אמיריקא ה' עליהם יחי' אלי'

אליכם אישים אקרא כי שמועה שמענו ונרעם כי אתם השרים וצאתכם הטוב הוא שאאמרו היושבים בעהק שיהיה להם פרנסה מעבודת הארץ
בזמן אבותנו הקדישים ואני רוחם עשיתי מעשה כאשר כבר הנדיני לכם לעבור : ושענגו המסתיר אולברט מאיעור עד קאמפיני באו ~
מתחילה לעג'ן ירושלים ת' נעשה להם המיסיונר ב' מעשולם כמה יעז ומן ותבזולות לימד היו תרשעים לכבר הכל והוריאו לבא פה
יעהק יפו ת' ומסיבה שבכבאן ער' המישזור ומים יש יכולים לעשות מלאכת הטובה ולימד את ישראל במלאכת הארץ הקדושה כאשר
המה כבד עוש'ב יש תחת ידם כמה בא מישראל עוסקים במלאכת הארץ ומתפרסים וגם שכרו ממנו הגינה של יען מתו ופרדות של
וחו היתה הולכת לאיבור ואם היה יהיה שכתבנו לכם איזה מכתבים או שמיעתם איזה שמועה לא טובה הלא תדע שכל אלו הדברים
אינם אלא על גי ד' משידם שהאמת הוא שאין עושה שום דבר טוב ל'ישראל כא לטובתו ולהאנה ולעאשן הוא דורש אבל האנשיב
האלה שלמים הם איתנו ומבקשים טובת ישראל ויש אצלם יהודים שעוסקים במלאכת הארץ ומתפרנסים על ידה וזרעונם הטוב לעשוירת
עוד טובה הרבה עד שיבא עד עזרה יען צריכים לקנות עוד שדות עשיע קריב לבנותם כדי שיעסקון בהם עד כמה בא ויחפרושו
וצריכים לבנות להם בתים כדי שישבו : כי על כן אנא דאמרי בבקשה ותחזו למעלתכם שתעזרונו ויצא מחשבתכם הטובה לידה
למועל כאשר עם לבבכם לכבבם הטוב והלכה והציב יימזד איתכם אסר ואם תרצו אתם השרים גם אני אתנעק עמהם בזה העניו ונשלח לכם
ישמות העזוקים במלאכה וכל מה שיתפר לישראל למען תאמינו שכל מה שדוברים רעה הוא זוקא על אנשים אחרים אבל יעל
אלו אין אנחנו יכולים לדבר כא טובה כא לש כדי נאה החתום פעהק יפו תובב"א כשא לה איר תרי"ד לי' וט

הצעיר רפאל
יאורה בכמוהור
מנחם הלוי הי'
פוח ומין
פעהק יפו
ת'

Letter (in Hebrew) from Rabbi Raphael Yehuda Ha-Levi to the Jews of the
United States, 1854. The letter is an appeal for donations to support Jewish
agriculture in the Jaffa region, with the ultimate goal of economic and religious independence for Jewish farmers. Courtesy of the Library of the Jewish Theological Seminary of America.

the course of generations was well understood, and after much
consideration, she and her colleagues had come to the conclusion
that to ameliorate the condition of the Jews in some lasting way,
a system of apprenticeship to agriculture had to be introduced.

Because he wished his people to engage in agriculture, Rabbi
Ha-Levi supported the American project. Although he had been
farming for some time and was hopeful that other Jews would join
him, he had run out of money and in July 1853 appealed to the Jews
of America to support the work of Mrs. Minor and her group,
saying, "I often visit them & rejoice to see that they progress well."
He pored over every issue of *The Occident, and American Jewish Advocate,* and recommended that a Hebrew edition be printed so he
could follow the progress of fundraising in America.

Rabbi Ha-Levi's support was due at least in part to the

Sephardic makeup of the Jaffa community, for the Jews of the Arab world did not have a history of persecution at the hands of Christians. Nonetheless, the subject of the Jewish response to benevolent Christian intervention is central. In early 1854 a major American Christian newspaper proclaimed that the Jews were interested in agriculture and regarded Christian efforts favorably. They realized that their poverty and oppression would be a permanent condition until they had employment of some kind, and they knew that agriculture was the best choice. Yet they knew nothing about it, nor did American Jews, and the American Jewish community conceded that teaching the Jews of Palestine to farm had to be done by Christians. Furthermore, the Jews and "wandering Arabs" hated and feared each other, and that hostility kept the Jews within the walls of Jerusalem. A third party was necessary to mediate between them, and indeed the little company of Americans farming in Jaffa had succeeded in bringing Jews and Arabs together to work the same garden. Their settlement offered hope that the hostility between the two peoples might be extinguished. The Jews were aware that Christian efforts to aid them would be coupled with an attempt to "help" them spiritually as well, but they were willing to hazard a try.

Several agricultural models were taking shape at the same time, and the main forum for discussing their respective merits was The *Occident, and American Jewish Advocate*. In September 1853, a few months after Clorinda Minor had gotten settled in Jaffa, a Jewish activist named Moses Sachs, president of the Agricultural Committee at Jaffa, wrote to Isaac Leeser asking for assistance—not for mere alms, but for "a perpetual source of benefits," namely agriculture. With ten Jewish families, Sachs was certain they could establish a farm in Jaffa, where freedom and security then prevailed, and where foreigners were permitted to pursue agriculture, whatever their religion. Land was very inexpensive, and already an American group, Mrs. Minor's, and several Prussians had bought a few gardens to cultivate. At the same time that Moses Sachs's appeal went out, Albert Minor requested support in the United States for his mother's undertaking, and Warder Cresson, an American farmer and convert to Judaism, was in the process of setting up a similar farm, first near Jerusalem, then outside Jaffa. Leeser felt that if Sachs's plan could be carried out by "American Israelites," with the experienced Cresson to oversee actual labor, it would be far better than anything that had yet been attempted to "improve the moral state of the poor of Palestine, whose occasional reported defection from our faith . . . is owing to actual starvation, to the absolute inability to obtain food, except through the missionaries . . . these self-same hunters of souls."

In a series of bold editorials, Leeser offered an extensive and astute analysis. Without agriculture or industry, the Jews of Palestine were forced to rely on an ultimately crippling system of support. "We are unable to form any estimate of the amount of charity which is collected throughout the world for Palestine; nor are we able to measure the ill effects which this almsgiving and receiving have produced for the last two centuries." Leeser did not blame those who gave, nor those who were compelled to receive. But "it is against the spirit of Bible and Talmud to depend solely on gifts of men, and to do nothing for one's support, on the one side, and to encourage such dependence on the other." Quoting Rabbi Gamliel, son of the editor of the Mishnah, who taught, in the Sayings of the Fathers (*Pirkei Avot*), that "all study of the law, which is not combined with labor, will at length come to an end, and will be the cause of sin," Leeser wondered what was the use of "idle students," who did nothing but read all their lives, depending on either pension or alms. Leeser was not sure if the rabbis discouraged agriculture, but he was convinced that "a new feeling has been infused in the masses," whereby they viewed indolence and its "consequent dependent state as an unbearable curse."

"The poverty of Palestine . . . is no fiction," he wrote, "it is a stern and painful reality." And if the charity did not arrive on time, the situation was even worse, as the Jews were forced to borrow from Muslims at 12 to 15 percent interest. He therefore questioned the wisdom of allowing any more aged and sick Jews to go to Palestine to live out their days, and he proposed a thorough reexamination of the whole system of *chalukah*, for it "has utterly failed to remove the direful load of poverty which weighs down the little energy which is yet remaining among the young and more vigorous." Realizing that he would be accused of lowering students of the Law to mere laborers, Leeser insisted he would put it otherwise —that he wished to see them thus elevated. The schools would not be diminished but would become more useful by operating "on a free, high-minded people, living by their own industry, instead of on a crushed, timid race, that shrinks before their oppressors into the smallest corner, for fear of exciting their wrath."

A forceful proponent of Jewish national revival, Leeser extended his argument well beyond an examination of the system of charity, or even of the benefits of agricultural colonies. Far ahead of his time, he cut an altogether new path by encouraging the Jews of Palestine to learn to use weapons for self-defense, that they might be able to stand up to their oppressors. Peace is the greatest blessing, he proclaimed, "but it is no peace where the proud oppress the humble." Long before the actual formation of Jewish self-defense societies in Palestine, he suggested that the Jews of Palestine organize themselves for mutual protection, if they could obtain permission from the sultan to form "regular companies of national guards" for the protection of their homes. If those who lived in the fertile plains were prepared for self-defense, their neighbors would learn to respect them, and Palestine would become a "thickly settled country, teeming with smiling villages and open towns." Leeser thus anticipated the two revolutionary aspects of political Zionism—the Jewish return to agriculture and the principle of self-defense.

Placing himself in a delicate position, Leeser sanctioned, even encouraged, the association of Jews with Christian missionaries. While he noted that various Christian societies on the scene were taking advantage of the helplessness of the Jews, others were encouraging their desire for independence by sending agriculturalists to employ Jews in farming "their own ancient home." If Jews themselves could have sent a sufficient number of "intelligent and practical Hebrew farmers" to teach agriculture, then the help of missionaries could be refused, but since that was not the case, it was senseless to turn away agricultural American missionaries, "no matter what their ultimate object may be." If the missionaries could do the practical good they proposed, "we . . . will not lay the smallest hinderance in their way." He himself did not especially fear the missionary threat, believing that "the poor, in accepting work from their benevolent teachers (for we honestly believe that their intentions are good), will resist all allurements to change their faith in the living God for a mediator who does not exist." Therefore Leeser advised Jews to put their suspicions aside and send money to purchase or lease land, repair ancient cisterns, and buy equipment. It was critical that the new Jewish farmers be taught that the "secular sciences" were not inimical to religion.

Leeser welcomed the day when hundreds of "sturdy" American farmers, mechanics, and machinists would go out and teach "the children of Judah how to labour, and how to live by their own exertions." If the Americans succeeded, they would have done more to lift the Jewish people out of poverty than all the "munificent sums" which had been sent "from time immemorial." Industry, he wrote, "is the thing wanting." For too long, the Jewish people had been the "prey of disunion and poverty." He urged Jews to hail the prospect, dim as it was, that feet other than those of "armed warriors, or fanatical pilgrims," would soon tread the soil of Palestine. He felt it was a pivotal moment in Jewish history and in the affairs of Palestine. The population of Palestine was growing; housing was becoming scarce in Jerusalem, Jaffa, and Beirut, and soon new structures would have to be built outside the walls of the cities, and new towns founded. Anticipating intense Jewish opposition to supporting missionary efforts of whatever sort, Leeser exhorted other Jews to join him in welcoming these "benevolent hearts" who feel for our people, "although their hopes are not our hopes; although their belief is not our belief."

As Leeser indicated, the ideal situation would be if Jewish farmers taught their skills to the Jews of Palestine. One of the projects for which his support was solicited was that of Warder Cresson, who, as farmer, convert to Judaism, and immigrant to Palestine, seemed the encapsulation of all that Leeser was looking for. Cresson was raised a Quaker in Philadelphia, but experimented with various sects as he sought the "true" religion. With a knowledge of Judaism gained through his acquaintance with Isaac Leeser, Cresson decided in 1844 to leave his large and successful farm, his comfortable life, his wife and six children, and go to Palestine. Through an influential friend, Cresson managed to have himself appointed the first U.S. consul in Jerusalem. When notice of his appointment was published, however, it outraged an eminent citizen who impugned Cresson as a religious fanatic who preached in the streets and was unfit for the post. The commission was subsequently revoked, but Cresson was already in Jerusalem, where he set up his consular office, as was described by the writer William Makepeace Thackeray among others. Cresson's "tenure" petered out over the next few years, and although in 1852 he made a half-hearted attempt to secure the appointment of vice-consul, his diplomatic enthusiasm had cooled.

In Jerusalem Cresson became more and more concerned with the desperate plight of the Jews, who were converting to Christianity out of need, not conviction, a view supported by a missionary who commented that out of all the Jews he had converted, he believed only one was a true Christian. Yet as Cresson became immersed in the suffering of Palestine Jewry, he was also arriving at the conclusion that Judaism offered him what he had been seeking. In 1848 he converted and was circumcised, taking the name Michael Boaz Israel. Thereupon he returned to Philadelphia to arrange his affairs so he could settle permanently in Palestine. His arrival home was hardly received with approbation, and his wife and son filed charges of lunacy against him. The case occupied two years, ending with his acquittal, the defense bolstered by the testimony of an expert who "proved" his sanity through hair-follicle analysis. It was clear to the most liberal people that, besides greed, it was horror at the thought of a rational man converting to Judaism that had precipitated the suit. Mordecai Noah, then a newspaper editor, helped Cresson's cause and declared that he could never believe "that a Christian Court would decide that adopting Judaism as a religion would be a proof of insanity."

Cresson stayed four years in Philadelphia, attending synagogue services and becoming known for his piety. In 1852 he made plans to return to Palestine to open a "Soup-House" for destitute Jews and to start a farm outside Jerusalem's walls. Though thought by some to be unstable, Cresson was perfectly cogent in his proto-Zionist argument that the Jews' condition of exile had sapped their energies, and that only territorial restoration could reinvigorate them. Less an organizer than a dreamer, Cresson did not pursue any of his projects beyond a short time. A year before the end of the Crimean War in 1856, Cresson had another idea. The Jewish philanthropist Judah Touro, from Rhode Island, had died recently, leaving Sir Moses Montefiore as executor of a sixty thousand dollar bequest for "relief of the poor in Palestine." Cresson heard it might be used to develop manufacturing in Jerusalem, but he felt it should be put towards agriculture, a much more salubrious way of life, morally and physically. He hoped Montefiore would buy a large tract of land in Jaffa, so that the money earned from agriculture would meet the hard times of "famine prices." Cresson remained in Palestine, marrying and having two more children, and died in Jerusalem in 1860. He was ungenerously described shortly before his death as "more Jewish than the Jews," and in his zealotry and fervently anti-missionary stance was said to be giving "a very bad specimen of a Jew."

The fall of 1854 brought Warder Cresson and Clorinda Minor within earshot of one another. Having decided to transfer his projected farm from Jerusalem to Jaffa, Cresson needed land, and what he found was a parcel belonging to David Clossen. The only problem was that the garden was then occupied by Mrs. Minor, Clossen's land having been the means by which she became established in Jaffa. Cresson did not have to do any finagling to replace Mrs. Minor as leaseholder, for Clossen had already decided to transfer it to him when the lease of the "American Conversion party" expired at the end of May. This pleased Cresson, who smugly remarked that Mrs. Minor's group would surely be disappointed, "just as they have gotten things so nicely fixed with 'The New York Society for Ameliorating the Condition of the Jews.'" This wresting of the land from her control brought Mrs. Minor to a precarious point, but she absorbed with equanimity what was tantamount to another eviction. For one thing, she had always dreamed of buying her own land, and Clossen's shift in allegiance thrust her in that direction. For another, she herself knew something of the inner life, and she must have intuitively understood that what was behind Clossen's change of heart was far beyond her power to challenge. In November, Clossen, soon to be called Abraham David, was in the process of converting to Judaism. After a visit to Jerusalem and dinner with Cresson, he summoned his fellow convert and requested that Cresson, who had undergone circumcision a few years earlier, be present at Clossen's own operation. The ceremony bound the two men, and Mrs. Minor bowed out.

Cresson's commitment to the development of agriculture in Palestine came late, given that he was a farmer and had been in Palestine for so long. The Soup House he had come to Jerusalem to establish was intended to induce the poor to work and end "this most miserable system of continual beggary," but he thought it would be better to invest in agriculture instead. "[O]ur moral state is extremely low, and what else can we expect, when a people are completely pauperised, and depend upon nothing but begging; proving our Talmud, most certainly true, which says, 'All the study of the law without handicraft will ultimately be futile and end in evil,' and is it not the case now with us?" Feeling that grown men were beyond training, he proposed to teach agriculture and silk-growing to boys ages fifteen to twenty, "and it may be the beginning of our physical redemption, and our 'spiritual' or rather moral, must follow, and not precede it as our good Christians erroneously declare." He cited alcoholism as one of the problems that would persist if Jews were not given work, and he affirmed that "a Jew will not steal if he only can get his necessities supplied."

Isaac Leeser continued to be occupied by the condition of the

Jewish community in Palestine. He hoped things would change, since the sultan had passed a decree that all non-Muslims were to be treated on an equal footing, thus giving Jews more freedom. But he cautioned that change would take time, because most of the Jews were either natives of Palestine or came from countries where no political freedom was offered to them, and where "contempt and oppression" were their daily fare. What was needed was a revolution in their domestic habits. As soon as the Jews saw that they could participate—could labor without fear of being plundered and could enter the competition that was spreading and bringing revitalization to Palestine—then they would ardently engage in the struggle for independence.

In early 1856 Leeser was still pressing for agricultural employment of the "idle and impoverished Jewish population of Palestine." Recalling his earlier intuition that the people were not voluntarily idle, and that the rabbis did not discourage industry, he was happy to report that a recent traveler to Palestine confirmed his feeling, noting that the Jews there were not only fully disposed to labor, but were willing to work for "the merest pittance." The subject of Jews working the land would become a permanent feature of Jewish discussion. It would surge, then ebb, for the next decades, and resurface of course at the end of the century, with new vigor and conspicuous results.

☾

For Palestine, the decade of the 1850s was marked by new projects and appeals, and optimism. The 1839 negotiations between Mohammed Ali, temporarily in control of Egypt, and Sir Moses Montefiore had to do with Mohammed Ali's desire for a large loan and Montefiore's interest in obtaining a charter for Jewish settlement in Palestine. Their contact generated numerous rumors of land purchases by wealthy Jews, and when Mrs. Minor

A Jewish cotton cleaner in Jerusalem. From *Picturesque Palestine, Sinai and Egypt*, ed. Colonel Wilson, R.E., C.B., F.R.S., with numerous engravings on steel and wood from original drawings by Harry Fenn and J. D. Woodward (New York: D. Appleton and Co., 1883), vol. 1, p. 44.

received word that the Baron de Rothschild was in Constantinople and had "bought *all* Palestine from the Sultan," she had no reason to doubt it.

In the meantime, Mrs. Minor's small colony was getting on slowly but with tangible results. Two more young Jewish men came to work for her and were learning English, and Mrs. Minor described the Jewish workers as having turned ruddy with the labor and fresh air. Her mood was elevated by the important news that the Chief Rabbi of Jerusalem had made a significant decision regarding the farm. It was the Jews' "sabbatical" year, the seventh year, during which the land was to lie fallow, as stipulated in Leviticus 25:1–4: "When ye come into the land which I give you, then shall the land keep a sabbath unto the Lord. Six years thou shalt sow thy field. . . . But in the seventh year shall be a sabbath of solemn rest for the land." Yet given the "existing circumstances"—whether that referred to poverty or the fact that the farm was in Christian hands—he had given permission to the Jewish workers to stay on. Mrs. Minor was enormously relieved, since one man had already left when the seventh year began, and she was afraid of losing them all. She renewed her plea for assistance, so that she could grab this moment, when a confluence of events seemed to make it the optimal time to engage in extensive agriculture in Palestine. If only "a few benevolent persons would unite and purchase a sufficient tract of this excellent land back of Jaffa for a Jewish colony, small or large, and keep the deed secured for such use."

Mrs. Minor's good standing is reflected in the fact that the American enclave was growing. In late 1853, Walter Dickson and his family came from Massachusetts and joined her in Jaffa. They did not know that their son Phillip, who had worked at Artas, had died, and that their daughter-in-law had sailed back to New England at the very time that the elder Dicksons were sailing eastward. Their plan was to work with Mrs. Minor, employing and aiding the Jews in agriculture. Dickson and his son were reported to be experienced farmers and mechanics, and immediately leased the other half of the garden the Minor group was working. With the land was a small house, but until they completed repairs and an addition, they lived with Mrs. Minor. Before long, one of Dickson's daughters was teaching a class of Arab children.

Just two weeks later, in January 1854, S. W. Jones, agent for "The American Society for Ameliorating the Condition of the Jews," arrived in Jaffa to look into the matter of introducing agriculture to the Jews. This was also the time that the unfortunate tug-of-war over the disputed house at Artas was being played out, and it was this Jones whom Consul Smith sent there. The simultaneity of those events—tearing down state seals, bolting doors, iron-plating windows, on the one hand, and cultivating new soil, on the other—highlights as much as anything the futility of the confrontation that almost squeezed the breath from their labor.

Jones and his wife had been sent out along with another couple, Charles and Martha Saunders, as the new mission of the Seventh-Day Baptists. Saunders was sent to organize agricultural work, Jones to tend to missionary matters; together, their new mission represented the first time that Mrs. Minor's coreligionists established a station alongside her. Saunders reported home optimistically that though prices were high because of the war, and thefts by soldiers who had deserted were common, investments would increase in value, and he saw the opportunity for "great usefulness." They celebrated their first Sabbath at Mrs. Minor's house with fifteen others, an emotional moment for their colleagues in the United States who had believed that the greatest mission of "Sabbath-keepers" was to establish a mission in the Holy Land.

Their daily routine continued to evolve. Dickson delivered the force pump that Mrs. Minor had requested, and Jones set to work with him to install it, a hazardous task given the well's great circumference and seventy-five foot depth. Once the bracing timbers were erected to secure the pipe and piston rod, the handle was attached, and up came water, to the amazement of the large crowd that had assembled to marvel at American ingenuity. Their irrigation method involved a long willow rope "bound thickly with earthenware jars" by which a constant stream was poured over the pulley wheel and conveyed to pools. They had a thriving fruit and vegetable garden and a mulberry orchard; their winter beets were prized by the Jews at Passover, their melons and grapes had to be the best in the world, and they raised sesame for oil. Their new American plow, a replacement for the one lost at Artas, was a boon because it dug much deeper than its Arab counterpart, and their wheat was five feet high. Their only personal discomfort was chilliness at night; the house had neither fireplace nor chimney, and they had sold their stoves the year before in Jerusalem when they were pressed for money. Mrs. Minor requested blankets to replace the ones they had brought, which were too tattered to be mended. By the spring of 1854 the war between Turkey and Russia was being fully fought, and though there had been some nervousness as it began, Mrs. Minor felt no real menace.

By then there were four places where Mrs. Minor's efforts were directed. One was a school for girls that Mary Williams and Emma Neil conducted. Next was the Dickson place, newly renovated, situated about a mile and a half north of Jaffa, in sight of their house and with adjoining wheat fields. Third was their own house, where they and "[their] Jews" resided, a place Mrs. Minor called their "first foothold here." If she was bitter when she learned that the Clossen lease would not be renewed, she kept it to herself. It had been her vision all along to buy land and establish a colony that would be theirs forever, and Clossen's betrayal was exactly the incentive she needed. Last, and most significant, was Rabbi Ha-Levi's garden, located further north, near the sea.

Six years earlier, in 1848, Rabbi Ha-Levi and a rabbi from Jerusalem had bought a twenty-acre piece of low-lying land and cultivated a large *biarrah*, which Mrs. Minor defined as "a watered fruit orchard." From an agricultural point of view it was successful, but because it was so far from the orange groves of Jaffa, Rabbi Ha-Levi couldn't safely employ Jews to work it. (When Jews worked for Mrs. Minor, they were considered to be under American protection.) Further, he could not manage the watering since all his mules had died, and he asked American Jews to send a pump, a device he had heard about from Mrs. Minor. Since her arrival, he had been asking her to take over his estate, but she simply could not stretch her resources that far. One day he came in great distress to say that Arab shepherds had broken a hedge and were pasturing their sheep among his fruit trees, and that his gardener had run away. Mrs. Minor held a meeting with Dickson and their German colleagues. The situation was urgent because the season was growing late, and all the earth between the closely planted trees needed to be hand-cultivated; yet their consul had cautioned them not to extend themselves any further from Jaffa than they already were. Beyond that, they could spare no workers. Lydia Schuler came up with a suggestion; if their Arab helper Abdallah (probably the same as had been sent to Artas with Jones) would go with her, she herself would watch over the *biarrah* temporarily.

Mrs. Minor regarded this crisis as the most profound test of their commitment. They were putting everything at risk if they agreed, and at just the time when they had finally begun to feel in control; but the meaning of their entire undertaking was trivialized if they refused. Realizing that their decision would send out a signal of the utmost importance, Mrs. Minor took a deep breath and plunged in. Her hope was to save Rabbi Ha-Levi's orchard and turn it into a "model farm" to which their elderly friend could retire in a year or so. Contiguous with Ha-Levi's land was a rich plain, "the finest site for a Jewish colony" Mrs. Minor had yet seen, and she wished the money could be raised to buy it. They

Working a well in a Jaffa garden. From *Picturesque Palestine, Sinai, and Egypt,* ed. Colonel Wilson, R.E., C.B., F.R.S., with numerous engravings on steel and wood from original drawings by Harry Fenn and J. D. Woodward (New York: D. Appleton and Co., 1883), vol. 2, p. 138.

trusted in God to aid them in "this truly first effort of the Jews themselves to cultivate this land!"

Rabbi Ha-Levi had introduced from Corfu the highly valued *etrog,* or citron, a citrus fruit that was essential to Jewish ritual at Sukkot. In one of his appeals to American Jews, Ha-Levi inquired what he could send in return for donations, and he offered their special kosher citrons, grown by Jews in Palestine. When he asked Mrs. Minor to take out a long lease on his land, he suggested that half the citron crop could serve as the annual rent. Her response to this suggestion was not recorded, but terms were quickly concluded, upon which she asked Ha-Levi for eight or ten Jewish laborers to break up the soil. He would have liked to send them, but they were so weak from their poor diet that they didn't have

A garden well, showing earthenware jugs. From Wilson, *Picturesque Palestine*, vol. 2, p. 81.

the strength to do such heavy work, though once the soil was broken, they could plant and weed. So the first week in March, two years after their arrival in Palestine, the Minor group set to work, along with Dickson, John Steinbeck, "[their] Jews," Abdallah, and eight neighboring Arabs whom they had hired out of necessity, but whose employment made for good relations all around.

They found Rabbi Ha-Levi's estate in miserable condition, and slowly they made improvements on the fences and buildings. Because of the distance from their home, they moved into a tent close to the fields. On the Jewish festival of Purim, in mid-March, a delighted Ha-Levi came out to see what had been accomplished. Trees had been thinned and transplanted, walks made, beds cultivated. Mrs. Minor continued pruning, while John Steinbeck and "the Jews" planted potatoes, corn, beans, and tomatoes. Water was plentiful, and the soil excellent. Reflecting on the promise held out by the land, Mrs. Minor wrote, "When weary, I sit down on the turf, under the young trees, now covered with their beautiful flowers, while the air is faint with their perfume, and watch the dark-browned, half clad forms before me." At such moments she thought that if true philanthropists could see them struggling with such a heavy but precious burden, they would surely come to their aid before the opportunity was lost to emancipate their suffering Jewish brethren. What this land was calling out for was "a well ordered agricultural colonial effort."

In late spring Mrs. Minor wrote a letter whose return address was the "Hebrew Biarrah, three and a half miles north of Jaffa." She was deeply contented, and was blooming under the spell of the sea, the fresh air perfumed by the blossoming orchards, the coolness of the morning and balminess of evening. The climate, often judged by westerners to be unhealthy, had been greatly misunderstood; a year at Artas, a season in Jerusalem, and nearly another year in Jaffa taught her that it was far more salubrious than any she had known. Because travelers suffered the privations of constant movement, and foreign residents lived in the crowded cities, they could never experience the pureness of the country air she had come to know. She explained that diseases of the throat, chest, and lungs, so prevalent in the United States, were absent in Palestine, and that most of them were in good health.

Their colony by then numbered sixteen Americans and ten Germans (counting children), and Mrs. Minor felt there was dizzying potential for growth. Jewish leaders from Jerusalem visited and expressed a desire to see the start of a real Jewish colony. Rabbi Ha-Levi spent a lot of time working with them, and his son-in-law, a scholar of Hebrew and Arabic, was teaching one of their newly arrived friends. Working with them were two young Jews, one with a wife in Jerusalem, the other with a family in Damascus. To another young couple, Mrs. Minor had given one of the best rooms, a little stone hut about fourteen feet square, like her own.

The soil of Palestine had been wrongly perceived as sterile. Even where it was rocky, around Jerusalem and Bethlehem, it produced grapes, figs, and olives. On the coast, they were surrounded by an expanse of rich earth, vacant except for an occasional Arab house, and yellow with wheat; north of Jaffa the land was as fertile as the western plains of the United States. The colony was increasingly productive, as they became familiar with the techniques of summer irrigation, and the Germans were successfully raising cattle, sheep, and goats. Mrs. Minor asked that such information be passed along, so that people would not regard their project as hopeless. Government officials showed them consideration, and an Arab neighbor was whipped for intentionally allowing his donkey to trample their wheat field.

Trying to quell anxieties at home, she insisted that no disturbances had been reported for several months, and they had found much to respect in "Mohammedan and Arab morality and manners." They had friendly relations with the Bedouin, who were generally "much feared and shunned" by Europeans. On one occasion she invited a sheikh to breakfast, and was invited to his tents in return, where their whole party, Jews and Gentiles, were well received. It was a memorable visit. She herself was an object of great interest to the women, as apparently they had never seen a "Frank face or dress!" She remarked that the sheikh would be regarded as "a superior person any where," handsome and richly dressed. In answer to her questions, he told her he disliked stone walls and preferred "a house of hair." Reflecting on her adventure, she wrote, "I could scarcely admit my own consciousness, when I saw such fine-looking, naturally intelligent persons, in such a migratory, uncivilized position, and that I was really in the midst of the wild Bedouins."

Mrs. Minor felt her experience would be of use to others whom she hoped would soon join them, and she made the case for acquiring land only, with no existing structures. Her group occupied houses and lands "arranged after the Arab fashion," an immense orchard with a garden, house, well, and machinery for irrigation. But the orchard needed to be "dug and watered" every summer, and demanded altogether too much care. Since leasing a house brought with it an orchard, she felt it was better for Americans to take empty land. She felt that the American way of laying out a farm would bring double the produce at half the labor. With as little money as they had, they had already established a worthy foothold, and most of the land was available for lease or purchase. Nothing prevented its being covered with "Jewish cottages" except lack of money, and not more than "a few thousand" would be adequate, if only people would come to their aid. Their hope was to buy a good piece of land where they could extend their farm, house their workers, and shelter the poor. Adjoining the *biarrah* which they were leasing were two hundred acres, and its proximity to the sea made it ideal. Elsewhere the soil was sandy or the tribes unfriendly; this large tract was fertile and was close to the newly improved Jerusalem road. Land value was increasing because of the war, and land was for sale to foreigners for religious purposes.

That summer it began to seem as if word of their labor might reach a large Jewish audience. Rumor had it that the Baron de Rothschild was prepared to invest a large sum of money in land to aid the poor. Rothschild's representative visited from Paris and expressed delight that Ha-Levi's *biarrah* had been transformed into a flourishing Jewish farm. One can almost see the changes for which the Americans were responsible. There were major repairs on the walls and gates of the farm, and five lower rooms and a stable were roofed and a second story erected. The cactus hedge had burgeoned, and six acres were under cultivation. Hundreds of citrus trees gave off a lovely fragrance, and they sold oranges in Jaffa daily. They had planted barley, wheat, lentils, beans, peas, and one peck of "American spring wheat." The year before they had planted only three "measures" of wheat on their small leased garden at Jaffa; this year they planted twenty, and Mrs. Minor was visibly proud of this milestone, that for the first time ever the soil of Palestine was being thoroughly broken up with American or European plows.

In spite of her unchecked optimism, however, a few disquieting details were creeping into the picture. When she acknowledged that the Germans were doing most of the work, she intended it as a compliment. The Bishop of Jerusalem, Samuel Gobat, however, was inimical to the colony's Sabbath-observance and wrote that the Americans were "handsomely subsidized from America . . . and reduce[d] the poor Germans to servitude," pressuring them to work all day Sunday and keeping the Sabbath on Saturday. More disturbing was the publication of certain articles at home. The missionary Jones protested vehemently about an article entitled "That Vandalism," in which, based on the views of James Finn, Mrs. Minor's character was assailed. Jones insisted that whatever course she followed in the past that gave suspicions, her conduct in the five months that he had known her was more than enough to redeem her. How cruel to see someone so innocent disparaged in reports from her own Sabbatarian press. Giving *The Sabbath Recorder* the benefit of the doubt, Jones allowed that maybe the report was "accidentally" printed. But as for the *Observer*—what evidence did the editor have to justify his saying that no one in the "so-called Agricultural Mission in Palestine" merited support? He hoped the writer of the article would repent for having held up "a lone, innocent female" to such abuse. Unpleasant as it was personally, the attack on Mrs. Minor represented a significant threat to the colony, whose existence depended on its reputation at home. Rabbi Ha-Levi, whose community had so much to lose, came to her defense, insisting that all the accusations were based on rumors spread by "the missionary Meshullam," who had never done anything good for the Jews, and had practiced "trickery and chicanery" on the Americans. Ominous from a very different angle was the visit of an American sea captain docked at Jaffa. He pressed two rifles on her for protection, and Mrs. Minor hung them on the wall, remarking that the very sight of them would warn off intruders, who sometimes came to "pilfer," an unsettling admission given her emphasis on their safety.

Mrs. Minor would not be swayed from her purpose by these distractions. There was only one major thought on her mind that fall as 1854 drew to a close, and that was permanent land acquisition. She was convinced that she would not be able to fulfill her mission until she had a large plot of land, with houses and individual gardens for their Jewish families, and she was intent on taking this next step. They were looking seriously at that time, and several small pieces had been offered to them. In February 1855, with a recent $500 donation, they made their selection, as she happily informed her son, and bought a large tract from a "native landowner." Mrs. Minor went into detail about the formality of the land sale. The American vice-consul Murad stood on the hill with them, asking the seller if he hereby sold to them the perpetual right and possession of this land, and asking them if they agreed to buy it. The whole process of drawing up and exchanging documents and observing formalities took six weeks, but Mrs. Minor was careful to take every possible legal precaution. The deed she received from the owner was sealed by the Turkish divan, and Mrs. Minor also obtained an official copy of the original grant from the sultan.

Given the prohibition on selling land to non-Muslims, Mrs. Minor expected that the deed would be made out in the name of a responsible "native" who would then turn it over to them, as had frequently been done when foreigners or Christians acquired land. But after the documents were delivered to her consul, she discovered that the deed had been made out in her own name, with the declaration that "it was the first deed ever thus made out to a Christian and foreigner in Jaffa!" She was obliged, in return, to supply a legally executed mortgage, in English, "in case of a Providential discontinuance of our work, through death, or unforseen calamities." Their neighbors were delighted and congratulated them on the purchase, saying that surely land value would rise. A Jaffa official said he had praised their work to the new pasha, who was just then assuming office in Jerusalem, and the pasha was so interested that he said he would recommend to the sultan that they be given every "privilege" necessary for the continuation of their benevolent work.

Their new thirty-three acre parcel was on a rise near the sea. It was two miles northeast of Jaffa, overlooking the city and the surrounding orange groves, with a view of the coast toward Mount Carmel. It had been planted with young grape vines, almond and apricot trees, and an orchard of five thousand valuable mulberry trees, all of which boosted its value. Mrs. Minor had also been offered the adjacent land, and she felt strongly that they should buy it before someone else did. But she knew it was not possible just then; most urgent was to construct a house before the lease on the original Clossen land expired that summer. As soon as the formalities were concluded, they immediately set to work, plowing between the trees, pruning the vines and almonds, and digging an irrigation ditch. Their pomegranates and peaches were flourishing, and they continued to sell oranges in Jaffa; they ate fresh produce every day, and they would "raise water" very soon. The wheat harvest was completed in June, and Rabbi Cohen, from Jerusalem, cut some to put aside for the following year's Passover, in fulfillment of Jewish law. They were at a double disadvantage for the threshing, without either oxen or a hard floor. But they had introduced the American pitchfork, which was a great help.

After the land purchase in February 1855, there is a silent period. It is hard to believe that sheer busyness would have prevented Mrs. Minor from writing, because even in the most stressful periods she had found time to correspond. Her letters had been her primary means of fundraising and, perhaps more than that, her only direct link to her son. Finally the silence was broken, with the last letter Mrs. Minor would write. It is dated September 1, 1855, and she was already ill. That there is no mention of her sick-

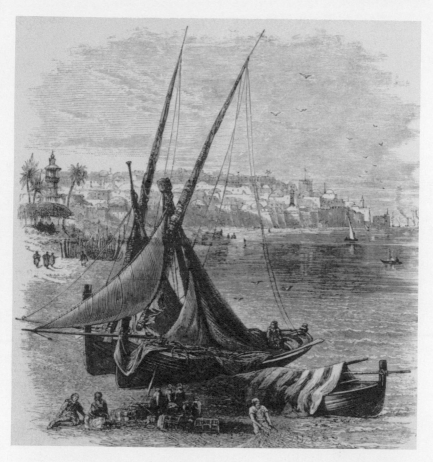

Jaffa viewed from the north. From *Those Holy Fields: Palestine, illustrated by pen and pencil,* by the Rev. Samuel Manning (London: The Religious Tract Society, 1874), p. 12.

ness in the letter may be attributed to her reluctance to admit to donors, more so to her son, that further funding should be suspended. More poignantly, her silence may have reflected her inability to admit that her body could not keep up with her spirit. Perhaps what we are seeing is the instinct to ignore the deepest messages of one's own constitution.

There was good reason for her to deny her illness, for it was a time of continued optimism about the future of the colony, primarily because of the potential participation of Sir Moses Montefiore. One morning Dr. Loewe, Montefiore's personal agent, rode up to Mrs. Minor's door with Rabbi Ha-Levi. They reported that Montefiore was in Jerusalem, where he had laid the cornerstone for a hospital on land he bought, had established a girls' school where students ages four to twenty-two could learn Hebrew, Bible, and homemaking, and had proposed a maternity facility. Reports had it that Montefiore was received like a prince in Jerusalem, that children danced in the streets before his entourage, and that he was widely considered a savior of the Jews. When Moses Sachs, founder of the committee to encourage Jewish agriculture, wrote dispiritedly that although Jews wished to farm, no plan for agriculture could yet be carried out because of "the weakness of the government and the barbarism of the country," he added that they must be patient, and in the meantime Sir Moses, surely the "chosen of the Lord," would continue his good works. Although the new pasha was trying to bring order to the land, Jews needed protection if they were to live outside the city walls, and Montefiore had a plan to provide thirty-five families in Safed, Tiberias, and elsewhere with a pair of oxen each, and to secure for them the right to sow land under the protection of the local sheikhs or governors.

In the next sequence of events, Montefiore bought Rabbi Ha-Levi's estate and hired Mrs. Minor to oversee it. Both of them recorded the transaction, but the tone differs considerably, depending on the point of view. According to Montefiore, when he arranged to buy the land, Mrs. Minor announced that she held a lease. She was willing to vacate, since she had just bought her own plot, but she insisted on payment for improvements she had made. The matter was settled, and Montefiore asked her to stay on for three months. From Mrs. Minor's angle, the exchange was far less perfunctory. She had been hoping Montefiore would buy land near hers for a Jewish colony, and she claimed that Dr. Loewe had told her that Montefiore was so impressed with her work that he had just bought Ha-Levi's estate. Dr. Loewe wished to know "what claims" were due the Americans, and how long it would take to give Sir Moses possession. Mrs. Minor was thrilled at this godsend; they would at last be able to turn their full efforts to their own new land, and Montefiore's involvement seemed to be the fulfillment of her greatest hope—that Jewish interest in agricultural pursuits would be aroused. Montefiore was not able to visit her himself, and he asked that Mrs. Minor come to Jaffa before his steamer sailed. At noon she went into town and visited the little Jewish hotel where the Montefiores were staying. Mrs. Minor wrote that she was received graciously and agreed to be reimbursed for half her expenses at Ha-Levi's farm, since the lease was only half-expired. Montefiore sought her advice about the continued operation of the *biarrah*, and he requested that she oversee his new estate until he found someone to replace her. This surprised her, but she agreed, and his wife Judith expressed gratitude for how Mrs. Minor had cared for the Jewish people. Saying goodbye, they expressed the hope that they would see her the following spring, trusting that "Providence would smile upon" the project Montefiore was beginning. There was a lot of work to be done, Mrs. Minor reflected, but her new home, which she called Mount Hope, was so close by that they would be able to continue farming at both locations. Whichever version of how their association came about is more accurate does not really matter. The fact that Mrs. Minor would live only two months more seems a grim and severe penalty to everyone involved.

☾

Clorinda Minor died on November 6, 1855, and those around her wrote long letters to her son, which, pieced together, open a window onto her last months. One of the condolence letters was addressed to Mrs. Minor's relatives, specifically to her "only son and adopted daughter," this being the first allusion to another child. Martha Saunders said she recognized that Mrs. Minor's health was declining for some time, and another one of the group dated her illness to early August. On the first of September she came down with chills and fever, then inflammation of the stomach and dysentery. Her physical suffering was severe and without interruption, and her companions were unable to move her. William Jones wrote that he had sent a note in the summer with "the girls," Lydia and Emma; the two women, loyal, if quiet, figures in the colony, departed because of poor health and took the news of their mentor's illness with them. Jones and his family had spent three months in Jerusalem; when they arrived back in Jaffa in early September, they found Mrs. Minor in bed, and they stayed to care for her for a week. Elizabeth Jones said she would bathe her and brush her long hair, and Mrs. Minor instructed that if she didn't get well Mrs. Jones should cut off her hair and send it to Albert and "tell him *all!*" She often spoke of him and said she would love to see her "boy" again, but that she mustn't think of it or it would kill her.

After a week, one of the Dickson daughters, Almira, took over. At first Mrs. Minor believed she would recover, and she considered staying in the Joneses' house while they continued work on her new home. But as the dysentery continued, she began to lose hope. When they asked her to see a French doctor waiting for the steamer in Jaffa, she said medicine would do her no good. In the middle of September she made her will, dictating it to Miss Dickson one night. They tried various remedies, but they gave only small and temporary relief. As she weakened, she said, "Tell Albert that I want him to come and continue this work." She was concerned about John Steinbeck, and asked the Joneses to comfort him, who had been like a son to her. By the end of October she was close to death. She was in "great agony," and asked how long she would live. She prayed a lot, and was concerned that the others were eating well. "We were all astonished . . . at the strength of her voice, and her appreciation of all things around her." A week before she died she said, "The fear of death has been taken from me since 1843," an apparent reference to the first Miller prediction from which she dated her new life. She remained fully conscious but was still in agony, and though she would have liked to live for the work's sake, she knew her death was the will of God.

Arabs and Jews and others who knew her were constantly asking after her. The Dicksons were kind, and the Saunderses were with her constantly for the last few days before her death. Rosa, "the colored girl," a previously unnamed member of the colony, also cared for her well. But John Steinbeck went beyond everyone in his faithful care, "as attentive . . . as any natural son could well be." He was Mrs. Minor's constant nurse, seeing to all her physical needs, carrying her and watching over her, anticipating every want with solicitude and tenderness. So impressed were the others that one of the members suggested to Mrs. Minor's son that Steinbeck be taken as an associate in the project. Martha Saunders, who was with Clorinda at the very end of her life, said that Mrs. Minor spoke about her belief that God approved the work she had chosen to do, and that she felt "unshaken confidence" in the final success of the mission. An hour before she died she called for Mrs. Saunders and asked to feel her warm hand on her breast. "I want to feel it, for death is cold—I am going." Then she called out, "Albert, my blessed child, my devoted Albert!" And she breathed more slowly, peacefully, and then stopped, at ten minutes before ten on the morning of the sixth of November. John Steinbeck broke out crying, "You are my mother," kneeling in grief by her body and crying that though she was not his natural mother, she was his mother who brought him to Jesus. Rosa and the "poor Jews" stood wailing, and after Mrs. Saunders laid her out, the "poor Arabs and Jews" came in "to mourn and weep together."

The next afternoon their colony assembled for the funeral at Mrs. Minor's house, in the same room she had built a little more than a year before. They were joined by several others, including the American vice-consul, Rabbi Ha-Levi, and their Jewish laborers. Dickson and his son Henry had made the coffin. The twenty-third Psalm, her favorite, was read in Arabic and sung in English. The men bore the coffin for burial at Mount Hope, her land. The grave was in a commanding place, near where Emma, Lydia, John, and Mrs. Minor herself had read and prayed before "the girls" went back to the States. Mrs. Minor was called "a woman of much prayer, strong faith, timid, yet showing remarkable energy of character." The headstone was inscribed with a passage from Romans: "Mrs. C. S. Minor, from Philadelphia, U.S.A., Industrial Missionary to the Jews. Died Nov. 6, 1855, aged forty-six years. 'She hath done what she could.'"

❮

While Clorinda Minor's efforts were for "the greater glory of Christ," she was not a missionary in the direct sense of the word. Though her stated aim was to bring the Jews back to the land in order to facilitate the Redemption, she insisted that the Jews of Jerusalem and Jaffa had approved of her efforts. "[T]hey *know* that we are not as missionaries, . . . that we do not labor for *hire*, . . . and they have . . . enjoyed the same liberty of conscience as we would righteously claim . . . for ourselves." Some Jewish leaders did accuse her of missionary intentions, but she denied it vehemently, acknowledging that she believed in Jesus Christ as the Redeemer, but that she had never made any attempt to proselytize and had discouraged others from doing so. On the contrary, she understood from "the appalling history" that Jews would be suspicious of Christian "interference," and she had hired only those Jews whom she judged to be most strict in their observance of the Sabbath and most devout in their prayers. Other Jewish leaders defended her, Isaac Leeser, himself Orthodox, foremost among them. Though he too believed that at heart she was a missionary, he praised her in an obituary: "She was a true friend of Israel. . . . By her practical labors in horticulture, feeble and lone woman as she was, she has proved that Palestine may be made to bloom again. . . . [W]hen the land of Israel again smiles with plenty and glows in beauty, let the name of its benefactress, Mrs. Minor, be remembered with a blessing."

Judgment of her work can only be made in the context of what was possible at the time: travel, communication, simple sustenance —these were major obstacles. Then there was suspicion, unfriendliness, hostility, both at home and in Palestine, and these must have created an atmosphere of uncertainty and at times dread. Yet Mrs. Minor persisted, for reasons that to a modern mind are nearly incredible. "We are here," she wrote, "to labor, to suffer, and, after spending our all, if God will, to perish, in the attempt to rouse . . . [a] profit-seeking world to emancipate from worse than American slavery the half-covered, starving, imprisoned, spirit-crushed Hebrew captives of Palestine."

What did Clorinda Minor remember as she lay on the earthen floor in her new home, on a coarse muslin-covered, corn husk-filled mattress? What did she think as the pain grew to occupy her utterly, demanded her most intense concentration, became her only future? Did she mourn her short life? Demand of her God the chance to see her work through to real fulfillment? Did she foresee the failure of the entire colony, which, held together by her immense strength and singular imagination, might have become one of history's great social experiments? Could she know that even in the few years given it, her settlement would come to serve as a model, and influence the Jewish social revolution embodied in the first Jewish agricultural settlements?

four

☾

The Aftermath

I T IS A SAD commentary on human endeavor that the Artas
dispute outlived Mrs. Minor. When Lord Francis Napier arrived a few months before her death to begin his investigation
into the Artas imbroglio, he interviewed Mrs. Minor, whom he
called the "principal mover in the whole speculation." With arbitration as the sole route out of the web, Meshullam chose a representative, but the Americans did not, and they refused to recognize
the appointment made on their behalf by Henry Wood, the new
American consul in Beirut. Perhaps they were being vindictive, because as a result of their refusal, the accounts remained unsettled,
tying up Meshullam's finances. It looked as though things would
remain that way indefinitely unless Wood was empowered to act
for Mrs. Minor. Intent on reconciliation, Wood wrote to Finn that
he hoped the English and Americans would never again quarrel in
Palestine.

Meshullam's life, meanwhile, had not returned to normal. His
original ground-floor eight-by-six room was in constant danger

of being flooded, since the three upstairs rooms had never been finished and were leaking. The previous year he and his wife and seven of their children were forced to take shelter in another room, but a spring burst one night under their bed, and they were driven out into the rainy darkness. The winter of 1856–57 was the wettest in memory, and still the Meshullams were not permitted to use the upper rooms. Finally, in early 1857, a settlement was reached. An English proxy spent a week in Beirut with Consul Wood, and the two arrived at a rather simple solution. Because all the Americans had either died or left the country, their affairs were considered bankrupt. Meshullam was invited to pay the remaining value of the house, which he did, and he received the keys.

In all, Finn figured that Meshullam recovered about a fifth of what the partnership had cost him, but his troubles were not over. Since the Turks had taken over the aqueducts four years earlier, the system had fallen into disrepair and water overflowed and flooded the farmland in the harsh winter of 1856. Meshullam was crushed by the sight of his work destroyed; his crops, the walls, the very soil were washed away. The Taamari Bedouin caught his vegetables floating down to the Dead Sea and sold them in Bethlehem. When Meshullam's son discovered men doing further damage the next day, he reported them. They countercharged that Meshullam was impeding public works, and the pasha insisted Finn punish him. Finn rejoined that Meshullam should be released from two years of taxes because of the flooding and should be appointed superintendent of waterworks. Further, he maintained that Meshullam deserved some reward from the Turks for his land reclamation.

From that time on, Meshullam's fortunes declined. Before long, probably because of his failed partnership with Mrs. Finn in a land purchase, his relationship with the Finns crumbled. The immediate issue was Meshullam's son Peter, who, as a youngster, had been Mrs. Minor's guide and translator on her first visit to Palestine. In 1858 the young man returned from serving under the British in Crimea and became close to the Finns. Both of them admired Peter, Mrs. Finn describing him as a modest young man with a soldierly bearing. Someone later commented snidely that to a man of Finn's "nervous temperament" and to Mrs. Finn's "masculine energy of mind," young Meshullam was "eminently attractive and useful," that is, that he was a remarkable and brave man whose qualities were lacking in Finn and were useless in his wife. (Finn's repeated forays to remote areas in order to defuse violence demanded courage that contradicts the remark.)

Finn hired Peter, but before long the young man began abusing his authority with the Arabs of the Artas region. It was said that Peter's elder brother Elijah, who lived off his parents, hated Peter and helped turn his father against him, but the abuses were undeniable. This iniquity was beyond the pale, and John Meshullam was forced to incriminate his own son. Charging Finn with complicity, he submitted that Peter had forsaken his parents and was oppressing his neighbors so badly that the family could no longer remain in the valley. Finn's response was to take Peter closer under his wing, promote him, and make him a partner in land they seized, according to Meshullam, from peasants in a nearby village.

Meshullam then tried to settle accounts between himself and Mrs. Finn, but she refused. When the accounts were deferred to arbitration, Meshullam lost; his request to pay in installments was rejected, and his property was attached. He feared the Finns' vengeance, and in self-defense he pressed charges with the Foreign Office in 1862, saying he was an old man with a large family, and was threatened with ruin after so many years of work. The letter was written in a neat script, obviously not his own; it was signed shakily, "J Meshullam."

As a result of the inquiry into his dealings with the Bedouin, Peter Meshullam was relieved of his office. But he had made implacable enemies among the Bedouin and the villagers. At just this time, in 1863, Finn's tenure as consul was ending. The change in consul, coupled with Peter's dismissal, emboldened the young man's enemies. He had spoken of his fear that death was close, and was suffering from poor eyesight and worsening health. Showing none of his former arrogance, he bitterly complained that he had been dealt with unjustly and had been thrown out into the world with no parents and no friends. A few days after writing that letter, Peter and Finn's son Alexander were out riding with a traveler they were taking on a tour. Peter's horse reared and he was thrown, twisting his ankle. His two companions rode to Artas for help, and he remained alone with his Arab servant. Alexander Finn reportedly saw three men, armed and disguised, lurking behind the rocks as he rode off, but he did not explain why he left his friend alone under suspicious circumstances. Peter was struck on the head from behind, the blow killing him. He was buried in the Protestant cemetery on Mount Zion. A suspect was arrested, but a year later the special Turkish commission investigating the death outraged the English by ruling that Peter Meshullam had died from his fall, though Alexander Finn testified that he had left him with only a sprained ankle.

All the controversy over Finn's finances resulted in his being replaced, and with Peter Meshullam's murder, the new English consul, Noel Temple Moore, took over. Moore was aghast at what he found in outstanding claims against Finn by both British and foreign subjects. A second investigation was ordered, but the report, like Napier's a decade earlier, basically rehabilitated Finn. His errors were not so egregious, and much of the enmity toward him was rooted in personal matters going back years, it was concluded. It was true that Finn could have made friends rather than enemies,

Jerusalem, looking west from Mount Scopus. From *Picturesque Palestine, Sinai and Egypt*, ed. Colonel Wilson, R.E., C.B., F.R.S., with numerous engravings on steel and wood from original drawings by Harry Fenn and J. D. Woodward (New York: D. Appleton and Co., 1883), vol. 1, frontispiece.

especially with the Anglican Mission; it was also true that his choice of the much-despised Peter Meshullam was a poor one. Because of financial difficulties he should have claimed bankruptcy, but the official did not blame Finn. Rather, his censure fell, perhaps with historical predictability, on the Jews: "The majority of his Creditors deserve no sympathy at all, and it would have been a good lesson to the Hebrew community here who have exacted their Pound of flesh and traded upon his difficulties." This official exoneration came too late to save Finn's job and perhaps his health and spirit too. It felt like exile when he left Jerusalem in 1863. He died nine years later.

❈

After Clorinda Minor's death in 1855, the colony that had grown up around her limped on. Her associates, though they shared her beliefs, did not possess her vision or her power of concentration, and it was not their objective to gain widespread support for their work. They continued farming quietly, stranded in a life that Mrs. Minor had invented, but which they never fully comprehended. Clustered together on the outskirts of Jaffa, three generations of Americans lived, farmed, and waited. Yet the end of their wait would be anything but divinely inspired, and the final days of their settlement would be defined by the harsh, all-too-human world.

In the fall of 1856, in the hope of physical and mental restoration, Herman Melville embarked on a voyage that would take him beyond Europe to the Levant. In January 1857 he arrived in Palestine for a month-long stay. In Jerusalem he met Warder Cresson, who was no longer farming at Clossen's estate and had given up agriculture. Cresson's conversion to Judaism and second marriage to a Jewish woman evoked a laconic comment of "sad" from Melville. (As the editor of Melville's *Journal* pointed out, Cresson appeared as Nathan, the American convert to Judaism, in Melville's immense poem, *Clarel.*) In Jaffa, Melville called on Charles and Martha Saunders. Melville's version of what remained of the colony is important because so few visitors passed through in those days, but his reconstruction of conversations he had there should be interpreted in the light of his disdain for Muslims, Eastern Christians, and Jews. Melville described Saunders as "a broken-down machinist," and saw the whole project as decidedly ill-conceived: "Might as well attempt to convert bricks into bride-cake as the Orientals into Christians. It is against the will of God that the East should be Christianized." They strolled in the orange groves accompanied by the elderly Miss Williams, while the Saunderses related to Melville the disappointing history of their Agricultural School for the Jews. The school had failed miserably because, in Mrs. Saunders's view, of the deceitfulness of the Jews, who would "pretend to be touched & all that, get clothing & then —vanish." At the moment, Saunders, his health ruined, was idle, and Mrs. Saunders studied Arabic and doctored the poor. The little Saunders girl longed for home, while her parents "waited the Lord's time." A year later, with the death of the American vice-consul Yacoub Murad, Charles Saunders was appointed to fill the vacancy.

Commenting on the wisdom of devoting one's energy to the Jews, Melville wrote that no Jew was ever converted—either to Christianity or agriculture. His prejudice obvious, his interest limited, and his logic questionable, he reflected with inadvertent prescience: "The idea of making farmers of the Jews is vain. In the first place, Judea is a desert with few exceptions. In the second place, the Jews hate farming. All who cultivate the soil in Palestine are Arabs. The Jews dare not live outside walled towns or villages for fear of the malicious persecution of the Arabs & Turks.—Besides, the number of Jews in Palestine is comparatively small. And how are the hosts of them scattered in other lands to be brought here? Only by a miracle."

Melville described Mrs. Minor as a "woman of fanatic energy & spirit," the first to teach agriculture to the Jews and whose example inspired others. But in a conversation with consul Henry Wood, Melville got a different impression, and he mentioned cryptically a "strange revelation" made by Wood concerning Mrs. Minor's "hidden life." Unfortunately he offered no details, only remarking that both Wood and Lord Napier, who had investigated the charges against Finn, thought she was a "crazy woman." The full story of the whispered charges brought against Mrs. Minor time and again during her short career will never be known. It seems that she could only have been excoriated because of her hidden relationship with John Boyd, her early companion. Whether or not theirs was a sexual liaison, it was certainly perceived as illicit. It is also possible that the charges were more mundane and had to do with either mismanagement of donated funds or outright embezzlement. Hovering over much of the correspondence relevant to the Artas affair is the suggestion that Mrs. Minor's personal integrity had been impugned. That might be why Mrs. Minor promised prospective donors that she would offer them a full and careful accounting of their contributions.

The whereabouts of Mrs. Minor's son Albert has been a puzzle. The fact that Melville did not mention him has to mean he was not there at the time of his visit, yet it has been suggested that Albert ran the farm after his mother's death. The only evidence of his return to Jaffa is a brief entry in Moses Montefiore's diary a few months after Melville's visit. Montefiore's assistant, Dr. Loewe, recorded that in May 1857 Montefiore visited the garden he had bought, inspected the newly planted trees, and examined the reports "handed to him by Mr. Minor." If Albert Minor came to settle his mother's affairs, it was a short stay; he did not continue her work, as she had hoped, for within half a year he was gone.

Saunders took Melville to visit Walter Dickson and his wife, their three daughters and son. Their farm consisted of twelve acres of mulberry, oranges, pomegranates, wheat, barley, and tomatoes. Melville described Dickson as "a thorough Yankee, about 60, with long Oriental beard, blue Yankee coat, & Shaker waistcoat." Invited into their "barn-yard sort of apartment," Melville talked with the Dicksons about their work. He asked if any Jews were working with him, to which Dickson answered no, he could not afford them. "Besides, the Jews are lazy & dont [sic] like work." But he went on to say that Christians had to teach them better, for the time had come. Mrs. Dickson asked if there was talk in America about her husband's work, and Dickson wanted to know if people at home believed in the restoration of the Jews. Melville had no answer, and the conversation trailed off. His concluding comment about Dickson was that he seemed to possess "Puritanic energy," was "inoculated with this preposterous Jew mania," and was "resolved to carry his Quixotism through to the end." The two elder Dickson daughters had married the Steinbeck brothers; Melville had little to say about them except that, married to Germans, they were "fated to beget a progeny of hybrid vagabonds." We can see him shaking his head in a mixture of bewilderment and disgust. "This whole thing is half melancholy, half farcical —like all the rest of the world." Sadly, the farce was soon to turn to tragedy.

When Mrs. Minor was living in Jaffa after the outbreak of the Crimean War, she observed that since the war with Russia, the "wild tribes" in the interior of the country had been involved in skirmishes with government troops. But her colony, she affirmed, continued to feel secure. Putting her faith perhaps in the symbolism more than the utility of the two rifles that had been pressed on her by the visiting American naval officer, she wrote, "We have *never* heard of their breaking into houses, or approaching where there are 'Frank' firearms, and they never take life except in revenge for a murdered relative."

The American and German settlements, intertwined by the relationship between Mrs. Minor and John Steinbeck, were knotted by the marriages of the young Steinbeck brothers, John and Frederic (wrongly reported by a Boston newspaper to be Jews) and the Dickson sisters, Mary and Almira. On arriving in Jaffa from Massachusetts at the end of 1853, the Dicksons farmed next to Mrs. Minor in a loose partnership with her. It was probably not before 1855 that the two marriages took place. Frederic Steinbeck married Mary Dickson, the couple eventually moving in with her parents. John and Almira lived near or with Clorinda Minor and remained at Mount Hope after her death.

Disaster came to the colony on January 11, 1858. Late that night three Arabs came to the front gate of the Dickson house asking about a stray cow. Dickson and Frederic Steinbeck, roused from bed, assured them it was not among their herd. After twenty minutes the men departed, but soon returned, calling out for Steinbeck. Frederic went to the gate, and they demanded to be let in, saying that Abdallah, at Clossen's garden nearby, told them the cow was on the Dickson property. They lay down at the foot of the wall, where they said they would remain until morning. Frederic went back to bed.

Meanwhile Dickson got a ladder and raised it to the eight-foot-high wall, climbed up, and peered over to see five men. In an attempt to frighten them off, he fired his double-barreled gun, which was loaded only with powder. Then he returned to the house, but after a few minutes, the dogs began barking. Dickson got up again, got dressed, and went out back, where he saw that the gate had been broken down, though no one had yet entered. By then Frederic was up and dressed, too. Dickson took the rifle down and gave it to his son-in-law. Together they went out back.

Steinbeck's wife later reported that Frederic had begun to load a revolver after the men threatened to break down the gate, but apparently didn't have time. It seems he took it outside with him anyway. Frederic spoke to the men in Arabic; then there was a shot. Steinbeck cried out he was hit and gave Dickson the gun. Dickson fired randomly and followed Frederic inside, where the young man cried to his twenty-four-year-old wife, "Oh Mary, I have got a ball." He went halfway across the room and collapsed on the floor before his wife could catch him. She held his head in her lap and opened his pants to the wound in the lower abdomen. She and her mother bent over him, trying unsuccessfully to stanch the flow of blood. Mary rubbed her husband's face while Steinbeck, suffering acutely, pleaded, "Oh Father, forgive all my sins, and help me to bear this dreadful pain." He lived another half hour.

By then it was after midnight. The family secured the doors and could do nothing more than wait. They heard a noise and realized the intruders were prying at the door from the bottom. The casing gave way, the door flew open, and the men rushed in, armed with guns and pistols, a sword and a seven-foot club. One of them struck Dickson on the head, and blood was running down his face as his daughter helped him to the back of the room. Dickson got up and tried to flee to give an alarm but was knocked down again. The assailants tore the funnel off the stove and pulled the weights out of the clock and, probably searching for money, forced Mary to open all the family's trunks. One of them jokingly put the younger sister's drawers over his head.

They grabbed Mary by the arm, but she seized the bedstead, and one of them struck her with the stock of his gun to release her hold. She resisted, tipping over the bed, where her eleven-year-old sister was huddled with Mary's infant son and little girl. They forced Mary outside, where they threw her onto the ground. One held his pistol to her and raped her, then another, then a third, after which the assailants went back to the house. The assault continued as another man dragged Mrs. Dickson into the adjoining room, tore away her nightgown, as witnessed by the eleven-year-old, and raped her.

Mary stumbled inside and knelt by Frederic, feeling in vain for a pulse. She sat down on the floor by her parents as the men ransacked the house, repeatedly demanding money. She curled under the table when they came for her again, but they dragged her into the other room and raped her again. One of the men asked why Frederic was sleeping on the floor, and when Mary didn't answer he struck her on the hip with a shoe-hammer and tried to take her wedding ring.

They continued to tear apart the house, threatening their lives. Dickson gave them his purse, insisting it was all the money he had. They asked him if he owned a mule and donkey, and held his head back as they took a swipe at him with the sword; his raised hand was slashed as he protected his throat. Another said they should kill Mary and get out of there. The men plundered until nearly daylight, taking all the bedding, clothing, carpets, money, food, and knives and spoons (leaving forks behind). Then they left. The family remained on the floor for another half hour. At daylight Dickson sought help. Charles and Martha Saunders came to the house and found Frederic on the floor in a pool of blood. Nearby, in shock, sat his mother-in-law and his wife, cradling the baby and little girl. The family moved into Jaffa, and by early spring were preparing to head back to the United States. In September, the Dickson and Steinbeck family sailed for America. They received two thousand dollars from the State Department for "repatriation."

After finding Frederic Steinbeck's body, Saunders rode to Jerusalem, and with the American and Prussian vice-consuls went to the pasha to report the violence. Pursuing justice fell to the U.S. consul in Jerusalem, John Warren Gorham, who had taken up his post just a few months earlier as the first American consul there. His appointment may have signaled a new alertness on the part of the United States following the Crimean War, but Gorham was hardly prepared for what he would encounter in the Dickson-Steinbeck case. A few days after the attack Gorham sent his official report to the U.S consul-general in Constantinople. The pasha had instructed the governor of Jaffa to do his utmost to apprehend the perpetrators, and Gorham, presenting the case to the governor, used "forcible, but not undignified, language." Avoiding explicit threats, Gorham made it clear that his government was outraged at the perfidy and demanded justice. Gorham offered a reward and hired secret agents to expedite the investigation.

From there, Gorham's superiors consulted with Captain Charles Bell, the naval commander of the American fleet at Alexandria, advising Bell that Gorham's authority would be enhanced by the appearance off Jaffa of an American vessel, the *Constellation*. Bell disagreed; since the authorities in Jaffa had agreed to investigate, he did not think a show of force was appropriate at the moment. If it became evident that they were "conniving," a ship-of-war could be sent within a few months, when the season was more favorable. The coast was a formidable one, and there was no safe anchorage at Jaffa, making Bell most hesitant to commit a ship that might have to sit for some weeks. Both the U.S. legation at Constantinople and Gorham regretted the decision not to intervene.

Writing to the secretary of state shortly afterwards, Gorham reported that a valuable witness had been permitted to escape, and American citizens in Jaffa and Jerusalem were in a state of "great agitation and alarm" because of the violence. In order to show them that their safety was assured, he ordered American flags to be raised at the consulates in the two cities, a decision not taken lightly, since showing the flag was meant as a sign of aggression. Indeed the pasha was more than perturbed; requiring an explanation, he described the act as an annoyance to the Sublime Porte. Gorham's private feeling was that the Turks were not acting in good faith, and that the numerous arrests they were making of non-suspects was intended to create a backlash of resentment against Americans and Christians.

After what Edwin de Leon, the American consul-general in

Egypt, called three weeks of "apathy, hostility, and treachery," the Americans succeeded in forcing the Turks to imprison four men, one of whom was known to be guilty, and to hold as hostage the sheikh of the fifth man's tribe until the man himself was turned in. At the end of February, the accused were lying in irons in the Jaffa prison, presumably awaiting orders for their execution, and Gorham was satisfied with the "so far successful termination of the affair." De Leon added that "if the matter is properly concluded, the American name will henceforward never be ignored, nor its people insulted or injured, while that memory remains with Turk, Arab, or Christian." Citing more than a dozen murders and uncounted robberies and rapes that had been committed in Jaffa in the last two years, and all with impunity, he concluded that if "a visible emblem" of American power—namely, a warship—had been sent out immediately, he had no doubt the whole business could have been resolved in two days rather than three weeks. He still felt that a ship should be dispatched, "to reassure the terrified Christians, to overawe the fanatic savages . . . and, finally, to insure the effectual punishment of those five bloodhounds of Jaffa." But Gorham evidently felt that the Turks were "trifling with him," and de Leon agreed. When he arrived in Jerusalem and was received by the divan, he effectively declared war on Turkey by refusing to take coffee and a pipe with his hosts. Asked by the governor if their respective countries were not at peace, de Leon replied no, that the Americans regarded murder and rape, "when permitted and screened by governors," as a declaration of war. Fortunately, the confrontation fizzled out.

As the incident was further investigated by the Americans, a broad field of danger signals was revealed. Giving evidence in early February, the Dickson family and John Steinbeck reported a sequence of hostile events that in retrospect appears so portentous as to make the tragedy that followed seem almost inevitable. Just

Public fountain at Jaffa. From *Picturesque Palestine, Sinai and Egypt,* ed. Colonel Wilson, R.E., C.B., F.R.S., with numerous engravings on steel and wood from original drawings by Harry Fenn and J. D. Woodward (New York: D. Appleton and Co., 1883), vol. 2, p. 137.

before the attack, Frederic Steinbeck and his wife Mary were living in a small hut within Steinbeck's enclosure, about twenty yards from the main house. One morning, while Steinbeck was in the fields and Mrs. Steinbeck was home with her younger sister Caroline and her two children, two Arabs (one either a soldier or dressed as one, the other a Bedouin) came to the door and asked for a light for their pipes. Caroline went to the main house to get "fire" from their mother. While she was gone, the soldier dismounted and approached Mrs. Steinbeck, who was described as fair and pretty, and touched her hair, as well as taking "other liberties." She knew Arabic, and he allegedly used "improper expressions" and asked if he could "sleep with her." The frightened Mrs. Steinbeck ran off to the other house, yelling to her father to get her husband. The Arabs rode off, but the soldier reportedly called back to her, "if you hear horsemen in the night don't be alarmed." Mrs. Steinbeck watched as the men rode off and saw them go to the second garden over from theirs. It was not the first time Mrs. Steinbeck had been approached rudely, but she had always been confident of her husband's ability to protect her.

The next morning John Steinbeck, her brother-in-law, went over to ask who the horsemen were, but he could not get any information. That night, the same men rode up to Steinbeck's house and demanded that he show them the road. He took his revolver and walked with them a short way, then, distrustful, turned back. One of the men blocked his way, drew a pistol, and ordered him to keep going. At that point an odd thing happened; one of the aggressors mistook the Dicksons' stovepipe for a man, and while he was distracted asking who it was, Steinbeck fired and yelled for Dickson's son Henry to come to his aid. The Arabs galloped off. As a result of these events, the Steinbecks moved back with the Dicksons, which is why they were there the night of the raid.

Four of the men who attacked that night had blackened their faces and were disguised. But both Mrs. Steinbeck and her young sister asserted that the undisguised leader was none other than the soldier, whom they recognized by both his voice and appearance. On the day that he intruded and expressed sexual interest in Mrs. Steinbeck, he told her that he was a Bedouin, and he named his tribe. But on the night of the assault, when she pleaded with him, saying, "I thought all Bedouins were our brothers," he replied that he was not a Bedouin, but from a village, and not her brother.

The investigation turned up other incriminating details. On the night of the killing, the assailants had so much plunder that they could not have gone very far; it was obvious that they only needed to walk the short distance to the neighboring farm, where they could hide the booty. The neighbor himself had a grudge against the Dicksons because he had just been arrested for stealing their sheep. He was undeniably aware of everything that had taken place, even if he had not participated; in fact his wife confessed that on the night of the killing, four men dined with them, leaving around midnight. When all the evidence was put before the grand divan, the men were apprehended, and the neighbor confessed his role.

That the attack was in large part a robbery seems without question; how much added incentive was supplied by the apparent infatuation of the leader with Mrs. Steinbeck can only be wondered at. But the rosy picture that Clorinda Minor had presented to donors is not borne out by evidence submitted by John Steinbeck, officially referred to as her "successor." Mrs. Minor had made light of occasions of "pilfering," but it seems there was some serious thievery taking place. To her, such incidents were relegated to the category of nuisance; because they revealed no pattern of hostility, she probably felt that publicity would do more damage than the incidents themselves. Still, in the four years between the fall of 1853 and late 1857, John Steinbeck detailed eight robberies and instances of intimidation occurring at three- to ten-month intervals. On several occasions donkeys and sheep were stolen or their house was entered and clothing and dry goods taken. Most painful to Steinbeck personally was the theft of his silver watch, a family heirloom. He judged that the settlement's loss amounted to at least seven thousand piastres, a considerable sum for which they never received any compensation. Yet more alarming to the community was that shots were fired at them during at least two of the robberies or robbery attempts; in one episode, Rosa, the young black American woman who lived with Mrs. Minor, was injured. The shooting incidents both took place in the spring and summer of 1855, just before Mrs. Minor became ill, when both her hopes and prospects were at their height. Her recourse to silence is doubly understandable.

By the end of March 1858, the American diplomatic corps felt they were about to achieve satisfaction in the Dickson affair. Indeed, the State Department believed the men had already been executed. Gorham reminded his superiors, without a trace of irony, that under Turkish law a trial had to be held first. Yet by June, nothing further had been accomplished. The Grand Vizier at Constantinople had instructed the pasha of Jerusalem to proceed, but the pasha was so often out of the city, whether quelling disturbances among the Bedouin, as he claimed, or escaping from them, that he had not attended to the directive. The five men were still in custody, but since there was no criminal court in Jaffa, it was decided they would have to be tried in Jerusalem when the pasha returned. Gorham was opposed to holding the trial there because he claimed the pasha was hostile to Christians. He argued for a move to Beirut, where there was a substantial Christian population

Bay of Beirut and mountains of Lebanon. From *Landscape Illustrations of the Bible, consisting of views of the most remarkable places mentioned in the Old and New Testaments, from original sketches taken on the spot*. Engraved by W. and E. Finden with descriptions by the Rev. Thomas Hartwell Horne, B.D. (London: John Murray, 1836), vol. 1, plate 27.

that exerted some influence, and a month later the defendants were transferred there.

Gorham had lost his patience and was clearly frustrated by this dilatory and circuitous route to justice. He repeated that if a warship had been available at any time during the last five months, the affair would have been brought to a close. If "barbarians" inferred that the consul was not supported by his government, there was no telling what further atrocities they might commit. Gorham said his own life had been threatened, as well as that of Murad, and he had warned all the local sheikhs that the responsibility for violence against Americans was theirs. (That summer an insurrection in Gaza was barely halted before violence against Christians took place.) James Finn believed it was crucial for the welfare of Christians that justice be meted out, but he felt that Gorham was not handling the case expertly.

The unfortunate Gorham was in over his head, through no fault of his own, and if his life wasn't complicated enough already, he was called on to answer to charges against his character and job performance. Gorham got seasick on the way to Beirut, resorted to brandy, and was subsequently accused of drunkenness. He insisted that he never drank, which is why the brandy hit him so hard. Besides the drinking, he was criticized for his management of what had become an interminable investigation, but in self-defense he inveighed against the pasha for his prolonged absence. He also had to answer for having had the trial moved to Beirut, and for neglecting his office in Jerusalem. It seems he couldn't win, and he was compelled to explain that the atrocity had made his presence in Jaffa necessary. The half year that had elapsed since the assault had taken a toll on Gorham, and it seems he had a kind of breakdown in Beirut. He explained it as having been caused by long anxiety, illness, and liquor, the last causing one to wonder if he was as unaccustomed to the stuff as he claimed. (He was relieved of his duties in September 1860 for alcoholism.) Yet Gorham's plight calls for sympathy; with neither precedent nor plan, he was isolated, and his closest advisors were in Alexandria and Constantinople. Until that moment, American diplomacy was largely untested in Palestine, and if the nation's first serious attempt at self-assertion in the haze of the Ottoman world failed, it is hardly a surprise.

In early fall, as the Dicksons and Steinbecks were embarking for the States, the trial was finally about to begin. But the court was not convinced of the guilt of all the accused, so Gorham and a committee were sent to Jaffa to make further inquiries. Unlikely as it seems, they actually obtained another confession and were led to the place where the Dicksons' belongings, including engraved silverware, were hidden. One of the accused was still at large, one was arrested on the basis of the new evidence, and two others were in prison in Beirut. Gorham, still smarting from the accusation that he had but feebly sought justice, felt restored; if he had pressed for an early trial in Jaffa or Jerusalem, all the prisoners, including the two guilty ones, would have been acquitted.

In an unrelated matter, but one that reflects on Gorham's mood and that of the Christian community, an Englishwoman was murdered in Jerusalem as she was going to visit the Finns. The five soldiers who were sent to arrest the Bedouin suspects were attacked. The captain was killed and cut into small pieces, Gorham reported, and three other soldiers were killed. The spared one was told to go tell his pasha that if he wished to take them, he should come himself and be treated as the captain had been and as the sultan himself would be. In a progress report to the State Department, Gorham observed: "It will be seen from these occurrences how very difficult it is to arrest the perpetrators of any crime in this country; and if to this difficulty is added the opposition of the authorities it becomes almost impossible. There is now only the shadow of authority in Palestine and this shadow is so attenuated by bribery and corruption that it has now become less than the shadow of a shade."

With the help of the testimony of a young Jew who worked at Montefiore's garden, confessions were finally obtained from the accused. One man cast the crime as a last-minute plot that did have to do with an ox or a cow, but given the evidence, that version is unlikely. It was more probable that the men had planned the robbery well in advance because they heard there was "a good job" to be done at the house of a European. Steinbeck was shot because he fired first, even though the gun was unloaded. Mrs. Steinbeck's statement was also confirmed by the confessions; some of the accused had gone to the farm on a prior occasion, Mrs. Steinbeck had given them water, and one of the criminals had asked her, in the words of the transcript, to sleep with him.

The wheels were turning at a maddeningly slow pace, and as they ground along, one of the accused escaped. Verdicts of guilty were delivered for murder, rape, and robbery, and Gorham said that the four still in custody would be executed as soon as they received orders from the Porte. The U.S. steam frigate *Wabash* made an imposing appearance off Jaffa around that time, but it was probably coincidental, and it had little effect on the proceedings. In the summer of 1859, Gorham was congratulated by the State Department for persevering. Two of the accomplices had been sentenced to life at hard labor, though no executions had taken place and the fifth man was still at large. An American ship landed at Jaffa, and Gorham accompanied its officer, Captain Levy, to an interview with the governor. The governor maintained he was doing all he could to apprehend the fugitive. Levy offered a substantial reward for information leading to the arrest of the man and cautioned that his government was losing patience and would not cease to pursue the affair, "even to extremities." In Jerusalem, Levy and Gorham had an audience with the pasha, who tried to explain the difficulties of tracking down a Bedouin and wondered why the American government was not satisfied with four of the five criminals.

A few days later Gorham was called on to examine a dead body that was loudly declared to be the very escapee whom they sought. The man, Gorham was told, had been killed two months before in a skirmish. Obviously the authorities didn't know that Gorham had practiced medicine and surgery for twenty years. It did not take him more than a glance to recognize the farce. The body, he pronounced, could not be that of the fugitive, for it had been dead close to a year, and the Turks knew that perfectly well. They shrugged their excuses, and Gorham left, certain that the governor of Jaffa alerted the fugitive when justice was closing in. Finally the Turks sent an officer to Jaffa, and he was busy arresting anyone who might know of the missing man's whereabouts, including his mother. Tracing the criminal to Acre, the officer ordered the pasha of Acre to arrest the man, but Gorham was sure that once again he would be warned in time to escape. So the Dickson affair dragged on. The Turkish government paid slight reparations, but it seems no one was ever executed, despite a report that one of the men was hung from the yardarm.

The attack had far-reaching implications. Notwithstanding the American consul-general's claim that numerous violent incidents had taken place in Jaffa in the last two years, James Finn noted that nothing like it had ever before happened to Europeans in Palestine. Even though the assault was motivated by theft, the experienced Consul Finn believed that the attackers must have had powerful backing. Some speculated that the intention was to discourage Christian missionaries, but Finn was sure that was not the case. Steinbeck was not a missionary, nor was Dickson, though he had come to Palestine out of religious conviction. In general, Finn felt missionaries had no special reason to feel endangered, and that to show fear was the worst thing they could do. More likely, thought Finn, it was done by those who wished to prove to the Turks that the Ottoman government could not keep order without their help. Still others interpreted the violence as a signal that foreign settlement of the country was unwelcome. The English vice-consul Kayat believed that the local authorities were subtly promoting acts of violence in order to discourage Christian settlers. As proof, he offered his knowledge of the pasha's secret order not to write any further land titles for Europeans and Americans. And since the order permitting land purchases was a recent one, it was easily rescinded. Mount Hope eventually ended up with the German Templars in 1869, eleven years after the violence that had closed the doors of the colony.

☾

Immediate justice is perhaps shorter-lived in the memory than slow injustice, and because of the belabored proceedings, the entire episode echoes as it might not otherwise have. By the end of the decade, the connection between the meandering investigation and the actual crimes was rather thin, and the continued urgency with which the Americans pursued the matter reflected far more than their desire for retribution. At stake was the image of the United States in the Ottoman world. Politically, America had only recently tiptoed onto the stage in Palestine, and immediately it was given a complex and demanding role. There had been no time for innocent experimentation. Citizens and interests had to be protected, power accumulated, and identity asserted.

But the memory of the American agricultural experiment, if dim, remains compelling. What is the justice that Clorinda Minor would have sought? Would the execution of the five men have satisfied her? Or would it have seemed a meaningless conclusion to her devoted work in Palestine? For finally there is the question of what Mrs. Minor's efforts meant; what lasting importance her colony had on the region, on the future settlement of Palestine, and on the nascent expressions of Jewish and Arab nationalism, aspirations that would be largely suppressed for another half century. Perhaps if the Jewish and Arab communities, under the influence of Mrs. Minor's Mount Hope, had found common ground before the route to mutual fulfillment and respect was lost in the maze of the twentieth century, the ensuing decades might have been shaped differently.

Jaffa, looking north. From *Jerusalem and The Holy Land Rediscovered: The Prints of David Roberts (1796–1864)* (Durham, N.C.: Duke University Museum of Art, 1996), p. 229. Courtesy of Duke University Museum of Art.

While it would be going too far to claim, as an English observer did in 1900, that Mrs. Minor was one of the first two Zionists (the other being Sir Moses Montefiore), it is clear from the records of early Jewish settlement that her example did help motivate Jews to consider farming in Palestine as a realizable enterprise. The *biarrah* that the Americans tended along with Rabbi Ha-Levi eventually passed into the hands of the newly formed Alliance Israelite Universalle, a French-Jewish philanthropic society. Their primary aim in Palestine was the establishment of Jewish agricultural settlements, and to that end they founded an agricultural training school, Mikveh Israel, in 1870. In 1878 the first Jewish settlement was founded at Petach Tikvah, followed by others in the next few years. Some of the first settlements did not thrive, but they were responsible for the development of yet others, this ripple-effect eventually leading to the kibbutz movement of the early twentieth century.

Mrs. Minor's work had implications in another arena as well. The competition engendered by the fight for Jewish souls had long-term effects on the division of power in the region. But in a curious way, that very competition, since it contributed to Jewish self-awareness, was a factor in the demise of the missionary network that was spread over Palestine. And it was the agricultural missionaries who contributed to the development of Jewish self-identity. As Jews learned what could be done with the soil they hadn't truly known in nearly two millennia, many realized also that waiting for the Messiah was not the path to national redemption. In the short time she had in Palestine, Clorinda S. Minor accomplished her goal—helping in the process of awakening Jews to their land, and thus to themselves. Without making larger claims than her work can bear, one can say that though she believed devotedly in the future, she lived passionately in the present. Her vision was beyond most of her contemporaries to fathom, but her work was daily work, physical and social. In this way her imprint remained for a long time in the new Jewish consciousness that was emerging and which would lead to political Zionism, the influx of Jews to Palestine, and the establishment of the State of Israel.

Which would it be—the Second Coming of Christian expectations, or the Messianic Age of Jewish hopes? For the Jews the difference was enormous. But to Mrs. Minor, it hardly mattered; it was a small difference between friends and would someday be settled. As she herself said, "We acknowledge . . . that we do believe that Jesus Christ is the Redeemer that shall come to

Zion, and that David will truly be raised up and be a prince over his people for ever. Israel believes also in the Messiah to come. This is future; let us labor in patient love and zeal in this good work of preparation, and wait until God shall . . . demonstrate his truth."

Sources and Chapter Notes

Introduction

Readers interested in pursuing various aspects of the background presented here will find an enormous selection of sources. For general literary and historical studies of the American experience in the Holy Land I recommend Lester I. Vogel's *To See a Promised Land: Americans and the Holy Land in the Nineteenth Century* (University Park, Penn.: The Pennsylvania State University Press, 1993), an impressive and highly readable examination of the American attraction to the Holy Land; it includes an exhaustive bibliography. Naomi Shepherd's *The Zealous Intruders: From Napoleon to the Dawn of Zionism—The Explorers, Archaeologists, Artists, Tourists, Pilgrims, and Visionaries Who Opened Palestine to the West* (New York: Harper & Row, 1987) examines the reawakening of the West's interest in the Holy Land. The relationship between travel in Palestine, Biblical archaeology, and American missionary efforts in the area is explored by Neil Asher Silberman in *Digging for God and Country: The Secret Struggle for the Holy Land, 1799–1917* (New York: Knopf, 1982).

Ruth Kark's *American Consuls in the Holy Land, 1832–1914* (Detroit: Wayne State University Press, 1994) is a very important study of the evolving American diplomatic presence in Palestine. Mordechai Eliav's *Britain and the Holy Land, 1838–1914: Selected Documents from the British Consulate in Jerusalem* (Jerusalem: Yad Izhak Ben-Zvi/The Magnes Press, 1997) offers a selection of hard-to-find documents, preceded by a very instructive essay of orientation regarding the British presence. David Finnie's *Pioneers East: The Early American Experience in the Middle East* (Cambridge, Mass.: Harvard University Press, 1967) remains a useful resource about the earliest days of the American connection to the Ottoman world.

The Arno Press has published an impressive series of more than seventy volumes that includes many reprints of nineteenth-century texts. It is invaluable for anyone studying the links between the United States and Palestine. The series was published under the aegis of the America and Holy Land project, with Moshe Davis as advisory editor.

Yaakov Ariel's *On Behalf of Israel: American Fundamentalist Attitudes toward Jews, Judaism and Zionism, 1865–1945* (Brooklyn, N.Y.: Carlson Pub., 1991), discusses the subject of millennialism in America. American millennialism and its peculiar relationship to Christian Hebraism is examined by Shalom Goldman in the Introduction to his edited volume, *Hebrew and the Bible in America* (Hanover, N.H.: University Press of New England, 1993).

Mordecai Manual Noah's "Discourse on the Restoration of the Jews" is included in a volume entitled *Call to America to Build Zion* (New York: Arno Press, 1977). The letters from Thomas Jefferson and John Adams are cited in Noah's Preface. Also included in that volume is an interpretation of the Book of Isaiah by Pastor John McDonald; presented in 1814, it is an argument for Jewish restoration to the Holy Land. Noah was one of the most interesting Jewish figures in nineteenth-century America. Jonathan Sarna's *Jacksonian Jew: The Two Worlds of Mordecai Noah* (New York: Holmes & Meier, 1981) is a highly regarded biography. Noah's life was marked perhaps most memorably by his proposal in 1825 to create an agricultural settlement for Jews in upstate New York.

The reader interested in early movements to restore the Jews to Palestine might go to the article "Zionism, Christian" in the *Encyclopedia Judaica* (Jerusalem: Keter Publishing House, 1972), which, in general, is an extremely useful and extensive resource. Barbara Tuchman's very readable historical study, *Bible and Sword: England and Palestine from the Bronze Age to Balfour* (New York: New York University Press, 1956) also examines this topic.

On the history and development of Zionist thought, I recommend Arthur Hertzberg's *The Zionist Idea* (New York: Atheneum, 1959). The articles on "Zionism" and the "State of Israel" in the *Encyclopedia Judaica* are of course very informative as well. Arnold Blumberg discusses the early Zionism of Rabbi Zvi Hirsch Kalischer in *Zion before Zionism, 1838–1880* (Syracuse, N.Y.: Syracuse University Press, 1985).

The intersection of the Jews and Protestant America is explored in Egal Feldman's *Dual Destinies: The Jewish Encounter with Protestant America* (Urbana, Ill.: University of Illinois Press, 1990). Feldman also discusses Mordecai Noah, as does Peter Grose. Grose's *Israel in the Mind of America* (New York: Schocken Books, 1984) examines the history of the idea of Israel in America from early times to the modern period. His first few chapters are of particular interest here. Gershon Greenberg's *The Holy Land in American Religious Thought, 1620–1948* (Lanham, Md.: University Press of America, Inc., 1994) is also an important contribution in this area.

The image of the Jew in nineteenth-century American society is the subject of Louise Mayo's *The Ambivalent Image: Nineteenth-Century America's Perception of the Jew* (Rutherford, N.J.: Fairleigh Dickinson University Press, 1988). Mayo points out that the Jews numbered a mere fifteen thousand in 1830, out of a population of fifteen million, but that by the late 1870s, after half a century of German-Jewish immigration, the figure was a quarter of a million.

Both the early version and the version that was finally passed of the Maryland "Jew Bill" submitted by Thomas Kennedy may be found in volume 1 of *The Jews of the United States, 1790–1840: A Documentary History*, ed. Joseph L. Blau and Salo W. Baron (New York and Philadelphia: Columbia University Press and the Jewish Publication Society of America, 1963).

Thomas Kennedy's remarks about Jewish restoration to Palestine may be found in an article by Louis Ruchames, "Mordecai Manuel Noah and Early American Zionism," *The American Jewish Historical Quar-*

terly 64 (March 1975): 195–223. Ruchames indicates that Kennedy's remarks were made in a debate around 1818, and he cites Moshe Davis, *Beit Yisrael Be-Amerikah, Mehkarim U-Mekorot* (Jerusalem, 1970).

One would certainly want to consult Isaac M. Fein's *The Making of an American Jewish Community: The History of Baltimore Jewry from 1773 to 1920* (Philadelphia: The Jewish Publication Society of America, 1971). See especially the chapter entitled "The Struggle for Equality," pp. 25–36. Fein provides references for all the speeches delivered about the "Jew Bill." He also points out that the Bill was at times contemptuously called "Kennedy's Jew Baby."

A central early work on the subject is E. Milton Altefeld's *The Jews' Struggle for Religious and Civil Liberty in Maryland,* originally published in 1924 (Baltimore: M. Curlander) and reprinted in 1970 (New York: Da Capo Press).

From the point of view of Jewish history, one might also consult *Religion and State in the American Jewish Experience,* by Jonathan D. Sarna and David G. Dalin (Notre Dame, Ind.: University of Notre Dame Press, 1997); and, in the series The Jewish People in America, *A Time for Gathering: The Second Migration, 1820–1880,* by Hasia R. Diner (Baltimore: Johns Hopkins University Press, 1992, American Jewish Historical Society).

In the context of early American history, one might see *Maryland: A Middle Temperament, 1634–1980,* by Robert J. Brugger, with the assistance of Cynthia Horsburgh Requardt, Robert I. Cottom, Jr., and Mary Ellen Hayward (Baltimore: Johns Hopkins University Press in association with the Maryland Historical Society, 1988). Brugger cites Fein's book, see above. Another useful reference is *Maryland: A History, 1632–1974,* ed. Richard Walsh and William Lloyd Fox (Baltimore: Maryland Historical Society, 1974). The chapter that is relevant to Thomas Kennedy is "Politics and Democracy in Maryland, 1800–1854," by W. Wayne Smith, who cites Edward Eitches, "Maryland's Jew Bill," *American Jewish Historical Quarterly* 60 (March 1971): 258–79.

An unusual further reference is an article by Robert Mehlman, "The Poems of Thomas Kennedy of Maryland," *Journal of the Rutgers University Libraries* 33:1 (1969): 9–19. Mehlman points out that in his battle to enfranchise the Jews, Kennedy was motivated by his devotion to the cause of freedom.

A particularly interesting related article is Isaac M. Fein's, *"Nile's Weekly Register* on the Jews," in *The Jewish Experience in America*, II, Abraham J. Karp, ed. (Waltham, Mass. and New York: American Jewish Historical Society and Ktav Publishing House, 1969), 82–101. Originally published in 1960, the article discusses editor Hezekiah Niles's sentiments in favor of equality for Jews and his musings on the question of their restoration to Palestine: "We know of no reason why a very numerous and severely oppressed people should not rise up and attempt to shake off the yoke of their obdurate tyrants. . . . It is easy to imagine that . . . they may . . . obtain for themselves the rights and privileges which they see enjoyed by others and to fix themselves a HOME and a COUNTRY. . . . The concentration of one-half . . . [of the world's Jews] . . . would . . . produce a strange revolution in the moral and political state of the world. . . . The deserts of Palestine brought into cultivation by patient industry may again blossom as the rose and Jerusalem miserable as it is, speedily rival the cities of the world for beauty, splendor and wealth" (*Niles Weekly Register* 11, Nov. 9, 1816, 168).

The same volume (see above) includes correspondence relating to the persecution of the Jews in Damascus in 1840 (pp. 266–280). Relevant documents are also contained in vol. 3 of *The Jews of the United States, 1790–1840: A Documentary History*, ed. Joseph L. Blau and Salo W. Baron.

The American Society for Meliorating the Condition of the Jews is one of the missionary groups described in David Eichhorn's *Evangelizing the American Jew* (Middle Village, N.Y.: Jonathan David Publishers, 1978). An essay on the effect of conversion attempts on American Jews is Jonathan Sarna's "The American-Jewish Response to Nineteenth-Century Christian Missions," in Naomi Cohen's volume, *Essential Papers on Christian-Jewish Relations in the United States* (New York: New York University Press, 1990). Sarna points out the name change of the American Society for Evangelizing the Jews and discusses the fear the Society instilled in the nascent Jewish community.

For a history of American Jews, I recommend Arthur Hertzberg's *The Jews in America: Four Centuries of an Uneasy Encounter* (New York: Simon and Schuster, 1989).

Chapter One

The significance of William Miller in American religious history has been widely discussed. Because the purpose here was to focus specifically on his influence on Clorinda Minor, no reference was made either to studies of Miller himself or to the Millerite movement as it developed after his death. His *Evidence from Scripture and History of the Second Coming of Christ about the Year 1843* was published in 1842 (Boston: Joshua V. Himes). One might consult Robert T. Handy's *A History of the Churches in the United States and Canada* (New York: Oxford University Press, 1977), or, for a brief reference, the *Dictionary of Christianity in America*, Daniel G. Reid, coord. ed. (Downer's Grove, Ill.: Inter-Varsity Press, 1990).

To recreate the fiasco of 1844, I have relied on eyewitness accounts which appeared in the *Pennsylvania Inquirer and National Gazette*, especially October 22–25, 1844. Commentary also appeared in the *Philadelphia Public Ledger* (October 11, 1844). In 1896, Clorinda Minor's papers came into the hands of one Jane Marsh Parker. Parker was initially cynical about Mrs. Minor, but as she immersed herself in the letters she began to feel an affinity with her: "Some twenty years ago, I became custodian of a package of old letters which had been collected with much painstaking, for the biography of a woman prominently identified with one of the great religious delusions of the century. . . . Just when . . . [the collector of the papers] . . . had reached the point of beginning at last the writing of his exhaustive biography—'Clorinda S. Minor; Martyr and Prophet of these Last Days'—he was called from this life, too suddenly to choose a custodian for his papers. In the settlement of his estate they fell to me, to my great dissatisfaction. Not long since, in clearing out the attic corner where those papers had lain undisturbed so long, my impulse to throw them into the rubbish basket was restrained by a sense of obligation to their collector. . . . What I resolved should be a hasty scanning became an absorbing reading. . . . The result is . . . this stray leaf from the history of a nearly forgotten but important fanaticism of the century." "A Fanatic and Her Mission," the four-part article that Jane Parker wrote, draws a sympathetic portrait. It appeared in *The Churchman*, beginning on October 10, 1896.

Virtually nothing is known of Mrs. Minor's life prior to her infatuation with Millerism, and even her own account, contained in her book, *Meshullam! or, Tidings from Jerusalem* (self-published, 1850; reprinted New York: Arno Press, 1977), offers very little by way of biographical information. The first part of this chapter is based to a large extent on her memoir, which I approached with both appreciation and skepticism. Wherever possible, other versions of events were brought in to balance her account. Mrs. Minor's portrait of Meshullam is contained in the Arno Press edition of her book, as are other important letters not to be found elsewhere, some from John Meshullam and others from various individuals connected to the activities of the German group at Artas. For a history of the Jewish community of Salonika, one might consult the *Encyclopedia Judaica*.

James and Elizabeth Ann Finn were no less given to highly subjective readings of events than Mrs. Minor was. Their accounts of life in Jerusalem are unquestionably central to any study of the region in the mid-nineteenth century. *Reminiscences of Mrs. Finn* (London and Edinburgh: Marshall, Morgan & Scott, Ltd., 1919), dictated by Elizabeth Finn some fifty years after she lived in Jerusalem, is a fragmented but fascinating memoir. Although details need to be checked, her recall is astonishing. For example Mrs. Finn notes that in 1854 the Askenazi community petitioned her husband to repair the old Khorvah synagogue, which became the biggest and finest synagogue in Jerusalem.

Also of interest is Mrs. Finn's fictionalized account of her life in Jerusalem: *A Home in the Holy Land: A Tale Illustrating Customs and Incidents in Modern Jerusalem* (New York: T. Y. Crowell, 1882). *Stirring Times, or Records from Jerusalem Consular Chronicles of 1853 to 1856*, by James Finn, edited and compiled by his widow (London: C. Kegan Paul & Co., 1878), is no less engaging, and also of great value. In *A View from Jerusalem, 1849–58* (Cranberry, N.J.: Associated University Presses, 1980), Arnold Blumberg has provided the consular diary of James and Elizabeth Finn with a thorough and extremely helpful set of annotations. An article by Sybil Jack, "Angels Come in Many Guises: Elizabeth Ann Finn, 1825–1921," in *The Woman Question in England and Australia*, ed. Barbara Caine (University Printing Service, University of Sydney, 1994, pp. 4–26) offers an interesting view of Mrs. Finn's life. I thank Ruth Kark for the reference.

The intertwining of American missionary and diplomatic history is the subject of Joseph L. Grabill's book, *Protestant Diplomacy and the Near East: Missionary Influence on American Policy, 1810–1927* (Minneapolis: University of Minnesota Press, 1971). The Jerusalem bishopric is the subject of Sybil Jack's article, "No Heavenly Jerusalem: The Anglican Bishopric, 1841–83," *The Journal of Religious History* 19, no. 2 (Dec. 1995): 181–203. Mordechai Eliav also discusses that subject in *Britain and the Holy Land, 1838–1914: Selected Documents from the British Consulate in Jerusalem*.

The reader interested in the connection between western nations and the Holy Land would want to consult the five-volume series, *With Eyes toward Zion*, edited by Moshe Davis. Particularly relevant here are the first volume, *Scholars Colloquium on America-Holy Land Studies* (New York: Arno Press, 1977); volume 2, *Themes and Sources in the Archives of the United States, Great Britain, Turkey, and Israel*, ed. Moshe

Davis (New York: Praeger Press, 1986); and volume 3, *Western Societies and the Holy Land,* ed. Moshe Davis and Yehoshua Ben-Arieh (New York: Praeger Press, 1991). Professor Davis also introduced a four-volume series, *Guide to American-Holy Land Studies, 1620–1948,* vols. 1–3, ed. Nathan M. Kaganoff and vol. 4, ed. Menahem Kaufman and Mira Levine (New York, Praeger Press, 1980, 1982, 1983, 1984).

Yehoshua Ben-Arieh's *Jerusalem in the Nineteenth Century: Emergence of the New City* (New York: St. Martin's Press, 1986) provides a very useful overview of the development and physical expansion of Jerusalem during this period.

A summary of settlement efforts in the mid-nineteenth century was provided by the Reverend J. E. Hanauer. His "Notes on the History of the Modern Colonisation in Palestine" was published in the *Quarterly Statement* of the Palestine Exploration Fund in 1900. Years before contemporary investigators were exploring the subject, the pioneering Israeli geographer Zev Vilnay wrote an article on the American group, "Christian American Settlers and the Jews of Palestine" (Hebrew), *Moznaim* 8 (1935): 69–75. A contemporary discussion of settlement efforts is Ruth Kark's article, "Millenarism and Agricultural Settlement in the Holy Land in the Nineteenth Century," *Journal of Historical Geography* 9, no. 1 (1983): 47–62. Rehav Rubin's "History of the Colonization of Artas," in *Zev Vilnay's Jubilee Volume,* ed. Ely Schiller (Jerusalem: Ariel Publishing House, 1984), pp. 325–30, gives an account of the settlement of Artas.

One of the truly fine books on life in mid-nineteenth century Palestine is Mary Eliza Rogers's *Domestic Life in Palestine* (London, 1862; reprinted London & New York: Kegan Paul International, 1989). Rogers had two lengthy visits to Palestine in the 1850s, when she stayed with her brother, who was British vice-consul in Haifa. She was what I would call one of the accidental travelers, women whose presence in Palestine was occasioned by the work of father, husband, or brother. With no professional agenda, these travelers were often far more open to experience than the men whom they accompanied.

Further, as women, they had access to the lives of both Muslim and Jewish women, and their accounts are literally irreplaceable. Mary Rogers's book is particularly intelligent and undoctrinaire. She shows perhaps unparalleled sensitivity to the women of the harem, and, though she spent far less time with Jewish women, she shows equal alertness to and empathy for them. She offers a significant, if brief, account, for example, of a school for Jewish girls established in Jerusalem by Sir Moses Montefiore.

Another very interesting account is *Hadji in Syria: or, Three Years in Jerusalem* (Philadelphia: J. Challen, 1858; reprinted New York: Arno Press, 1977) by Sarah Barclay Johnson, daughter of the American missionary doctor James Turner Barclay. Johnson is much less patient with Muslim women than Mary Rogers, and her attitude toward both Muslims and Jews reflects her missionary upbringing, but her book is an important contribution to the literary accounts of women. Like Mary Rogers, Sarah Johnson lived in Palestine around the same time that Clorinda Minor did.

I also recommend two somewhat earlier narratives, one by a young American lawyer, the other by his British counterpart. John Lloyd Stephens, the American, wrote *Incidents of Travel in Egypt, Arabia Petraea, and the Holy Land* (New York: Harper and Brothers, 1837; reprinted Norman: University of Oklahoma Press, 1970, and Mineola, N.Y.: Dover Publications, 1996). Alexander Kinglake, who traveled at exactly the same time as Stephens, took several years longer to write his book, *Eothen, or Traces of Travel Brought Home from the East* (London, 1844; reprinted Marlboro, Vt.: Marlboro Press, 1992 and Marlboro Press/Evanston, Ill.: Northwestern University Press, 1996).

Inner Jerusalem (New York: E. P. Dutton & Co., 1904), by Adela Goodrich-Freer, provides a spirited early twentieth-century perspective; see especially her lively chapter, "Cranks in Jerusalem." Philip Baldensperger, son of one of the German farmers at Artas, wrote a well-known and important book, *The Immovable East: Studies of the People and Customs of Palestine* (London: Sir Isaac Pitman & Sons, Ltd.,

1913). About Philip's father and the three other Germans who were involved in the Artas project, one observer predicted that all the young men would make lasting marks on life in Palestine. Schick became an expert on underground Jerusalem; Palmer served with Bishop Gobat; Muller encouraged the people of Bethlehem to plant vineyards, and Baldensperger assisted Meshullam.

The introduction of various crops to Palestine is a fascinating subject. Some travelers claimed that the potato was unknown in Palestine until John Meshullam's experiment, but in *Fifty-Three Years in Syria*, by Henry Harris Jessup (London: Fleming H. Revell Co., 1910, in two volumes), we learn that the potato was introduced, at least in northern Palestine, earlier in the century: "Rev. Isaac Bird introduced the potato in 1827 . . . and it has now become a universal article of food throughout Syria." The Americans' sweet potatoes and corn did represent first introductions of these crops. Sarah B. Johnson observed that "the American colonists . . . [have] . . . eminently succeeded in the cultivation of every article introduced by them except the apple."

The story of Dona Gracia and her attempt to resettle Jews in Palestine and start a silk industry is told by Cecil Roth in *The House of Nasi: Dona Gracia* (Philadelphia: Jewish Publication Society of America, 1947).

Chapter Two

An excellent travel account of the mid-nineteenth century is *Narrative of a Journey through Syria and Palestine in 1851 and 1852* (Edinburgh: W. Blackwood and Sons, 1854), by the Dutch traveler C. W. M. Van de Velde. Van de Velde's acquaintance with John Meshullam was brief, and his indebtedness to him may have colored his observations. Nonetheless, his view seems less biased than others, and his chance encounter with Mrs. Minor's group offers a unique glimpse of the Americans' arrival in Palestine.

Edward Robinson's 1838 sojourn in Palestine resulted in *Biblical Researches in Palestine, Mount Sinai and Arabia Petraea* (Boston: Crocker and Brewster, 1841). It is regarded as the cornerstone of modern exploration of the region. *Later Biblical Researches in Palestine, and in the Adjacent Regions* (Boston: Crocker and Brewster, 1856) is also a central text in nineteenth-century Biblical geography. His remarks about the Americans, though scanty, provide one of the few views of the group that we have from uninvolved parties. It was Henry Baker Tristram, in *The Land of Israel: A Journal of Travels in Palestine* (London: The Society for Promoting Christian Knowledge, 1865), who commented on the innovation of the wheelbarrow.

Clorinda Minor's correspondence is the best source of information about her group's activities. Many of her letters, to her son and others, were reprinted between November 1853 and April 1855 in *The Sabbath Recorder*, the newspaper of the Seventh-Day Baptists that had been in existence since 1844. For small related items one might consult the *Seventh Day Baptists in Europe and America: a series of historical papers written in commemoration of the one hundredth anniversary of the organization of the Seventh Day Baptist general conference: celebrated at Ashaway, Rhode Island, August 20–25, 1902* (Plainfield, N.J.: American Sabbath Tract Society, 1910). See vols. 1 and 2. *The Presbyterian*, the publication of the Presbyterians, also carried Mrs. Minor's letters between June 1853 and November 1855. The latter publication was sympathetic to her cause, but disapproved of her observance of the Jewish Sabbath.

Isaac Leeser's editorials appeared regularly in *The Occident, and American Jewish Advocate*. Jonathan Sarna discusses Leeser in *Jacksonian Jew: The Two Worlds of Mordecai Noah*. Valuable information is also found in *The Jewish Chronicle and Hebrew Observer*, between November 1854 and March 1856.

For a Jewish traveler's view of the Jews of Jerusalem, see Ludwig A. Frankl's *The Jews in the East* (London: Hurst & Blackett, 1859; trans. Rev. P. Beaton, two vols., Westport, Conn.: Greenwood Press, 1975). It was Frankl who remarked sardonically on the decor of the Anglican Church and the use of Hebrew (see vol. 2). Mordechai Eliav, in *Britain and the Holy Land, 1838–1914: Selected Documents from the British Consulate in Jerusalem,* commented on the conspicuous failure of the whole missionary enterprise in Jerusalem, noting that by the end of the nineteenth century, after sixty years of efforts, a mere 450 Jews had been converted. Eliav's book also offers a valuable summary of James Finn's career. The last chapter of Naomi Shepherd's *The Zealous Intruders* also offers interesting observations on the conversion issue.

Because Ruth Kark's *American Consuls in the Holy Land, 1832–1914* examines the subject from the beginning through the rest of the century, it places J. Horsford Smith in the context of the evolving American connection to Palestine. The study is thorough and indispensable.

J. Horsford Smith's official complaints about James Finn were directed to Washington and can be found in the United States National Archive, microcopy T367, roll 2. His version of events does not coincide exactly with that of his co-complainants, whose statements are also to be found in that source.

In the files of the Public Record Office in London, a portrait of the English consul James Finn emerges from his consular correspondence. See especially FO 195/369, for correspondence during the years 1851–53, for correspondence with and complaints of J. Horsford Smith, for the pivotal petition of the Jewish group, and for a copy of the contract between Mrs. Minor's group and John Meshullam. One might also refer to Finn's consular records, *Stirring Times, or Records from Jerusalem Consular Chronicles of 1853 to 1856.*

Lord Francis Napier's massive investigative report is in File FO 78/1138. The Napier report of January to May 1855 is perhaps the single most important document to anyone trying to decipher the breakdown of relations at Artas. Napier wrote his 112-page report, his penmanship careful, on both sides of pale blue stationery, with wide left margins for appendix references. The 600 pages of appended documents can all be found elsewhere, but Napier assembled them for convenience.

Vivien D. Lipman's book, *Americans and the Holy Land through British Eyes, 1820–1917: A Documentary History* (London: author, 1989) offers a brief but important summary of critical moments in these years.

See vol. 3 of *Guide to America-Holy Land Studies* for items related to the alleged misuse of American funds at Artas by John Meshullam.

Land acquisition by non-Ottoman subjects is a complex topic that has been extensively investigated by Ruth Kark. See her *American Consuls in the Holy Land, 1832–1914*. Professor Kark has also written an article that looks specifically at the village of Artas: "Land Purchase and Mapping in a Mid-Nineteenth-Century Palestinian Village," *Palestine Exploration Quarterly* 129 (1997): 150–61. In her article, "Changing Patterns of Land Ownership in Nineteenth-Century Palestine," *Journal of Historical Geography* 10, no. 4 (1984): 357–84, Professor Kark points out that even as far back as the 1830s, the Jews of Palestine were suggesting to Moses Montefiore and others that they buy land in Palestine.

Chapter Three

No study of Jaffa in the nineteenth century would be complete without Ruth Kark's book, *Jaffa: A City in Evolution, 1799–1917* (Jerusalem: Yad Izhak Ben-Zvi Press, 1990). The book looks at the economic, social, and political development of the city as it grew from a nondescript town to one of the centers of activity in Palestine.

A view of the settlements at Jaffa is contained in Shoshana Halevi's article (in Hebrew), "The Montefiore Orange Grove," *Cathedra* 2 (1977): 153–69. Biographical information about Rabbi Yehuda Ha-Levi comes from the two above sources, as well as from *The Encyclopedia Judaica*. Rabbi Ha-Levi's own description of his estate and his plea for assistance, both irreplaceable, are found in two letters (1853–54) contained in the Abraham J. Karp Collection in the Jewish Theological Seminary Library in New York.

Dr. James Barclay served as missionary in Jerusalem from 1851 to

1854. His book is entitled *The City of the Great King* (Philadelphia: J. Challen, 1858).

A great deal has been written about Isaac Leeser. Here, I used only his editorials in *The Occident, and American Jewish Advocate.* They are of inestimable importance in assessing reaction in the American Jewish community to Mrs. Minor's efforts on behalf of the Jews of Palestine. The discussion about the condition of the Jews of Palestine can be followed in the pages of *The Occident* and also in *The Presbyterian. The Jewish Chronicle and Hebrew Observer,* a London-based newspaper, carried correspondence relevant to the subject as well.

Samuel Gobat, who became bishop of Jerusalem when Bishop Alexander died suddenly, offers a missionary's view of these years. See *Samuel Gobat, Bishop of Jerusalem: His Life and Work* (New York: Thomas Whittaker, 1885). Gobat reviled the Clorinda Minor colony for reducing the "poor Germans to servitude."

There are two important articles that tell the story of Warder Cresson: "The Zionism of Warder Cresson," by Abraham J. Karp, in *Early History of Zionism in America,* ed. Isidore S. Meyer (New York: American-Jewish Historical Society, 1958), pp. 1–20, and "Quaker, Shaker, Rabbi: Warder Cresson, The Story of a Philadelphia Mystic," by Frank Fox, *The Pennsylvania Magazine of History and Biography* 95 (1971): 147–94. Cresson's own book is *The Key of David* (Philadelphia, 1852; reprinted New York: Arno Press, 1977). Although it is not what one would call a highly readable work, it is at times fascinating, as for example when Cresson details the confrontation between himself and his family concerning his mental health. The document also includes his refutation of the charge that he attached himself to "Shakers, Mormons, Campbellites, Irvingites. . . . then became a Millerite, and, lastly, an Israelite." One might also see William Makepeace Thackeray's portrait of Cresson, in *Notes of a Journey from Cornhill to Grand Cairo* (New York, 1846). Cresson's relationship with Mordecai Noah is examined briefly in Jonathan Sarna's *Jacksonian Jew: The Two Worlds of Mordecai Noah,* where Sarna cites Noah's defense of Cresson.

Cresson reported on Clossen's conversion and the simultaneous transfer of the garden: "I was sent for saying that he was going to be circumsised [*sic*] at Dr. Keil's and wished me to be present. I saw the rite performed, he offered me his gardens for the sum of 1500 piastres for one year." The above letter was dated Nov. 27, 1854, and was conveyed by the editor of the *Asmonean* to *The Jewish Chronicle and Hebrew Observer* (Aug. 3, 1855). It is interesting, given his background, that Cresson never made his mark as a farmer in Palestine. In *The Key of David*, he reminds those who accused him of "wasting his estate" that he had bought two farms (in Philadelphia) "which were nothing but poor *miserable* WRECKS; these I put good buildings upon [and] made them rich as gardens."

After Mrs. Minor's lease on the Clossen land was not renewed, she must have felt as though a second Artas were being visited upon her. Cresson was accused of living off the money for the poor, and of merely talking about leasing a garden in order to raise more money, but he insisted he could prove he had actually leased it. The accusations were vaguely linked to the Americans, though the source was never identified. *The Land of Promise: Notes of a Spring Journey from Beersheba to Sidon,* by Horatius Bonar (New York: R. Carter and Bros., 1858), is also of interest. It was Bonar who disparaged Warder Cresson, warning him that he was offering "a very bad specimen of a Jew."

The connection between John Steinbeck's grandfather and Mrs. Minor is mentioned in Jackson J. Benson's biography *The True Adventures of John Steinbeck, Writer* (New York: The Viking Press, 1984). A more recent biography is Jay Parini's *John Steinbeck* (New York: Henry Holt, 1995). A letter from Frederic Grosssteinbeck, John's brother, appears in Clorinda Minor's book, *Meshullam! or, Tidings from Jerusalem.* Dated November 20, 1850, from Jerusalem, it tells of the arrival in Palestine of the Grosssteinbeck brothers in 1849 from the Rhine province of Prussia.

The Diaries of Sir Moses and Lady Montefiore, edited by Dr. L. Loewe, vol. 2 (Chicago: Belford-Clarke Co., 1890) offers an important gloss on the years in question. The entry for May 17, 1857 mentions the visit by Charles Albert Minor. Also extremely important is the manuscript variation 21 II, in the collection of the National Library in Jerusalem. The entry for August 28, 1855, establishes Montefiore's formal connection to Clorinda Minor.

Concerning the absence of Albert Minor from Palestine, *The Occident* published a report in August 1854 (vol. 12, no. 5) entitled "Relief for the Distressed of Palestine." In it, Isaac Leeser noted that he received a communication from Mrs. Minor, "through the kindness of her son, who is now in this country."

Mrs. Minor's correspondence in *The Sabbath Recorder* and *The Presbyterian* remains central to the reconstruction of the events narrated here. Her colleagues' condolence letters to her son after her death appeared in *The Sabbath Recorder* from January to March 1856. Isaac Leeser's obituary of Mrs. Minor appeared in *The Occident* (vol. 13, 1856).

Mrs. Minor may have portrayed her circumstances as more serene and productive than they were in order to garner approval and of course donations. Yet her optimism was warranted not only by her reception by the Jews of Jaffa, but also by the Arabs, who were prepared to allow her to work their land. In fact she claimed that a great deal of prime land was available for either lease or sale, and that both Muslim and Christian landowners in the area begged them to settle permanently among them. Leasing was permissible, but purchasing land was another matter. Often, when non-Muslims believed they had bought land, what they had actually bought was the right to use the land and reap the harvest from it. Land sales were controlled by the Turkish authorities, and if Mrs. Minor's claim was accurate, as it seems to have been, it represented one of the first times that foreign Christians were allowed to buy land in Palestine. Although the laws were not rewritten until 1867, changes in land-acquisition regulations started to be introduced in 1856.

The account that Mrs. Minor gave of her purchase of land roughly corresponds to the account we have of another land purchase by a Christian woman. Mary Rogers witnessed the procedure followed by Mrs. Finn in buying a piece of land at Artas in May of 1856: "Ten of the fiercest and wildest-looking Arabs I had ever seen were assembled in the office of the Consulate, with their chief, a tall, powerful man, called Sheik Saph. . . . Mrs. Finn came forward and stood in the midst of the group of men, and said: 'O Sheik, do you agree to sell?' and Sheik Saph answered: 'I agree to sell, O my lady; do you agree to buy?' and Mrs. Finn replied: 'I buy, O Sheik.' Then the purchase-deed . . . was read over, signed, and sealed." Mrs. Finn's feeling was that she purchased land so easily because she was a woman, and women didn't count. Ruth Kark's work on this subject is ongoing. One would want to consult her article, "Changing Patterns of Land Ownership in Nineteenth-Century Palestine." Arnold Blumberg has also written about the subject in *Zion before Zionism, 1838–1880.*

Chapter Four

Mary Rogers visited the Meshullams at Artas in the summer of 1855 —after things had settled down, and before both the disastrous winter that followed and the deterioration of Meshullam's relationship with the Finns. She observed that most of the gardeners at work were Jews, and she offers a view of life there that sounds quite tranquil. Rogers comments that Meshullam's fruit trees and vegetable gardens were so prolific that he maintained a shop in Jerusalem to sell the produce. Everything was thriving, "especially the seeds and slips from America."

The litigation over the settlement at Artas is covered in the Public Record Office file FO 78/1295 (1857). Material pertaining to John Meshullam versus Consul Finn is contained in file FO 78/1712. James Finn's personal finances were investigated in 1863; the report is in the Public Record Office, file FO 78/1951. His financial failures were examined by Mordechai Eliav in "The Rise and Fall of Consul James Finn," (Hebrew) *Cathedra,* no. 65 (Sept. 1992): 37–81. Ruth Kark points out, in *American Consuls in the Holy Land, 1832–1914,* that as late as 1909, James P. Meshullam, of Newark, New Jersey, had requested that the U.S. State Department help him find out what happened to his parents' property at Artas. The investigation turned up nothing.

The Peter Meshullam affair, his abuse of power and murder, are contained in files FO 78/1952.

Herman Melville's trip to Palestine is recorded in his *Journal of a Visit to Europe and the Levant: October 11, 1856 to May 6, 1857,* ed. Howard C. Horsford (Princeton, N.J.: Princeton University Press, 1955).

The story of the Walter Dickson family is partially told in *The Groton Historical Series: A Collection of Papers Relating to the History of the Town of Groton, Massachusetts,* by Samuel Green, vol. 2 (Groton, 1890). The episode is examined again in *More People and Places of Groton,* by Helen McCarthy Sawyer (Littleton, N.H.: Sherwin Dodge Printers and Publishers, 1987). Statements that were taken from the Dickson family and a transcript of the eventual trial are found in the United States Senate Executive Documents, 1857–1858. The London Public Record Office file FO 78/1384 contains British documents pertaining to the crimes.

John Steinbeck discovered his family connection to Palestine and wrote a brief piece in *Newsday* (Feb. 12, 1966), p. 3W in which he created a bit of confusion. Referring to the diaries of his grandmother and his great-aunt Carrie, he related that the youngest Dickson daughter was grabbed by sailors as the family neared Boston, and was "so mauled that . . . she died soon after the ship landed." His grandmother recalled that the crew was "overfriendly." The murder aboard the Boston-bound ship is mentioned also in the Jackson J. Benson biography, *The True Adventures of John Steinbeck, Writer.* Is the report of this murder an error? As far as we know, the youngest daughter, who witnessed the rape of her mother and older sister in Jaffa, was eleven-year-old Caroline, who must be that very great-aunt Carrie. In Groton, Massachusetts, on one side of the Dickson family tombstone, is an inscription for Caroline Samuletta Danks, 1847–1932; it appears after that to read: "Daughter of W. Dickson." Eleven years old at the time of the violence in 1858, Caroline would have been born in 1847 and died at age eighty-five. Ruth Kark visited the cemetery and passed this information on to me.

I am grateful to the late Moshe Davis for pointing out that according to documents in the U.S. National Archive, Mount Hope was occupied by various people after Mrs. Minor's death. In 1869 the German Templars received the land from Mrs. Minor's "agents." It was evidently put in German hands rather than given to her heirs so that its original purpose would be maintained. One might also see "Introducing Modern Agriculture into Nineteenth-Century Palestine: The German Templers," by Naftali Thalmann, in *The Land That Became Israel*, ed. Ruth Kark (Jerusalem: The Magnes Press/New Haven: Yale University Press, 1990), 90–104. Ruth Kark (in *American Consuls*) also follows up on the final settlement, more than forty years after her death, of Clorinda Minor's estate.

Mount Hope, described by Clorinda Minor as being two miles north of Jaffa, is located not far from Tel Aviv's Central Bus Station. In the 1930s, Zev Vilnay located a small cemetery that had grown up around Minor's own grave, but both her tombstone and the cemetery disappeared in the next decades. It would no doubt please Clorinda Minor that a vocational school came to occupy the site.

Today one can stand by the breakwater of the port of Jaffa. Strong waves slap the shore, occasionally sending spray over the wall. The old town rises steeply and denies easy access. Few doors open to its winding alleys, making it nearly impossible to climb up to obtain a longer view. But no matter; one can turn to the west and look out at the endless light-flecked surface of the Mediterranean, and wonder what it felt like to wait for a ship, and a word from home.

Index

British consulate in, 3, 72
Chief Rabbi of, 61, 126
Jewish Quarter of, 32–33, 35, 86
Jews of, 3, 33–35, 64–65, 67, 112, 116, 144
Jewish restoration, 3, 4–6, 8, 35, 88, 121–22 155, (176, 179)
Jews of Palestine
  and attitude toward agriculture, 61–64, 116–20, 121–24
  and charity, 33–34, 114, 117–20
  and conversion issue, 35–36, 63–65, (186–87)
  competition for influence on, 81–82
  poverty of, 33–35, 37–38, 114–15
(Johnson, Sarah Barclay, 184, 185)
Jones, Elizabeth, 142, 143
Jones, William (or S. W.), 101, 127, 129, 136, 142, 143

Kalischer, Zvi Hirsch, 6
Kayat. See Jaffa, British vice-consul at
Kennedy, Thomas, 7–8
King Solomon. See Solomon, King

Leeser, Isaac, 63–64, 116–20, 123–24, 145
Leon, Edwin de, 159–60
Leviticus, 126
Levy, Captain, 168
Loewe, Dr., 140, 141, 154
London Jews Society. See London Society for the Promotion of Christianity among the Jews
London Society for the Promotion of Christianity among the Jews, 35, 43, 67

Manual Labor School of Agriculture for the Jews in the Holy Land. See Agricultural and Manual Labor School in Palestine
Marcy, William, 100

Maryland Jew Bill, 7
McCaul, Alexander, 35–36
(McDonald, Pastor John, 176)
Melville, Herman, 59, 152–55
Meshullam, Elijah (son), 29, 32–33, 43, 60, 92, 149
Meshullam, James (son), 29, 43
Meshullam, John, 27–29, 31–32, 37, 38, 39, 49, 51–52, 55, 56, 58, 64, 71, 73, 104, 136
  and Clorinda Minor at Artas, 56–61
  decline of, 147–49
  and petition, 82–88
  portrait of, 40–45, 46–47
  and tension at Artas, 65–67, 68–69, 90–103
Meshullam, Mrs. John, 30–31, 32, 43, 51
Meshullam, Minor, and Company, 92, 103
Meshullam! or, Tidings from Jerusalem, 13
Meshullam, Peter (son), 29, 45, 51, 148–50, 151
Messianic Age, 172
Michael Boaz Israel. See Cresson, Warder
Mikveh Israel, 171
millennialism, 4, 14, 16–17
Millennium, 4
Miller, William, 3, 14, 16–17, 143
Millerism, 14–17
Minor, Charles Albert, Jr., 18, 19, 50, 51, 52, 70–71, 82–83, 95, 98, 99, 101, 114, 117, 142, 143
  and contract with Meshullam, 60
  departure and absence from Palestine, 90, 96, 100, 154
Minor, Charles Albert, Sr., 17–18
Minor, Clorinda S., 9, 13, 38–39, 49, 55, 56, 57 64, 72, 73, 81, 109, 134, 135, 147, 149, 155, 163, 170–73, (180–81, 184)
  life of, prior to Palestine: